The Healing Art of Anime

A Coloring Book for all Ages

Created by Lauren Marturano Thompson

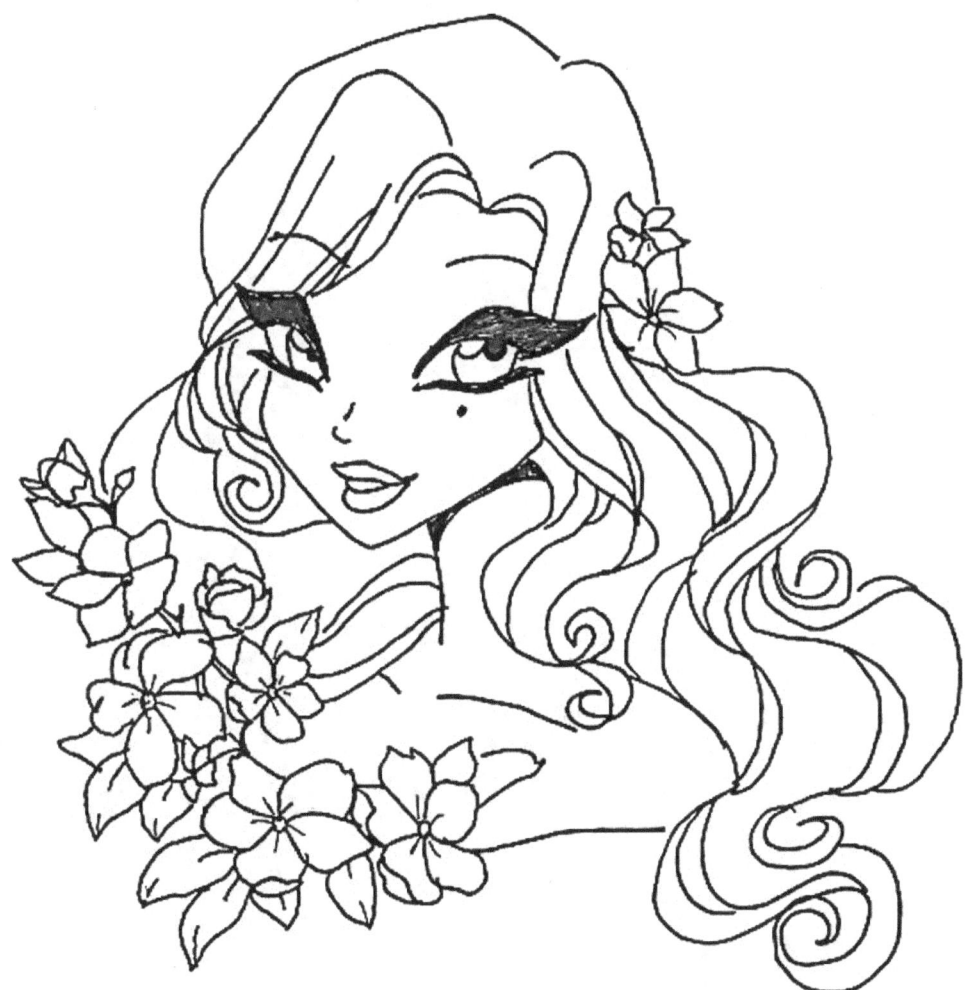

Forward:

I was not born dexterous, I was born with a physical disability. Simple things were not so simple. As for art, my mother could not even get me to pick up a crayon when I was a child. Not because of lack of interest, but because my physical disability made it too hard to draw. Today, I am an Anime artist, confident enough in my skill to publish this book. It is my hope that those with challenges will find this book and, through the healing art of coloring anime, learn to see the possibilities in life. Everyone has challenges, some are just more obvious to the outside world than others. Enjoy!

Lauren

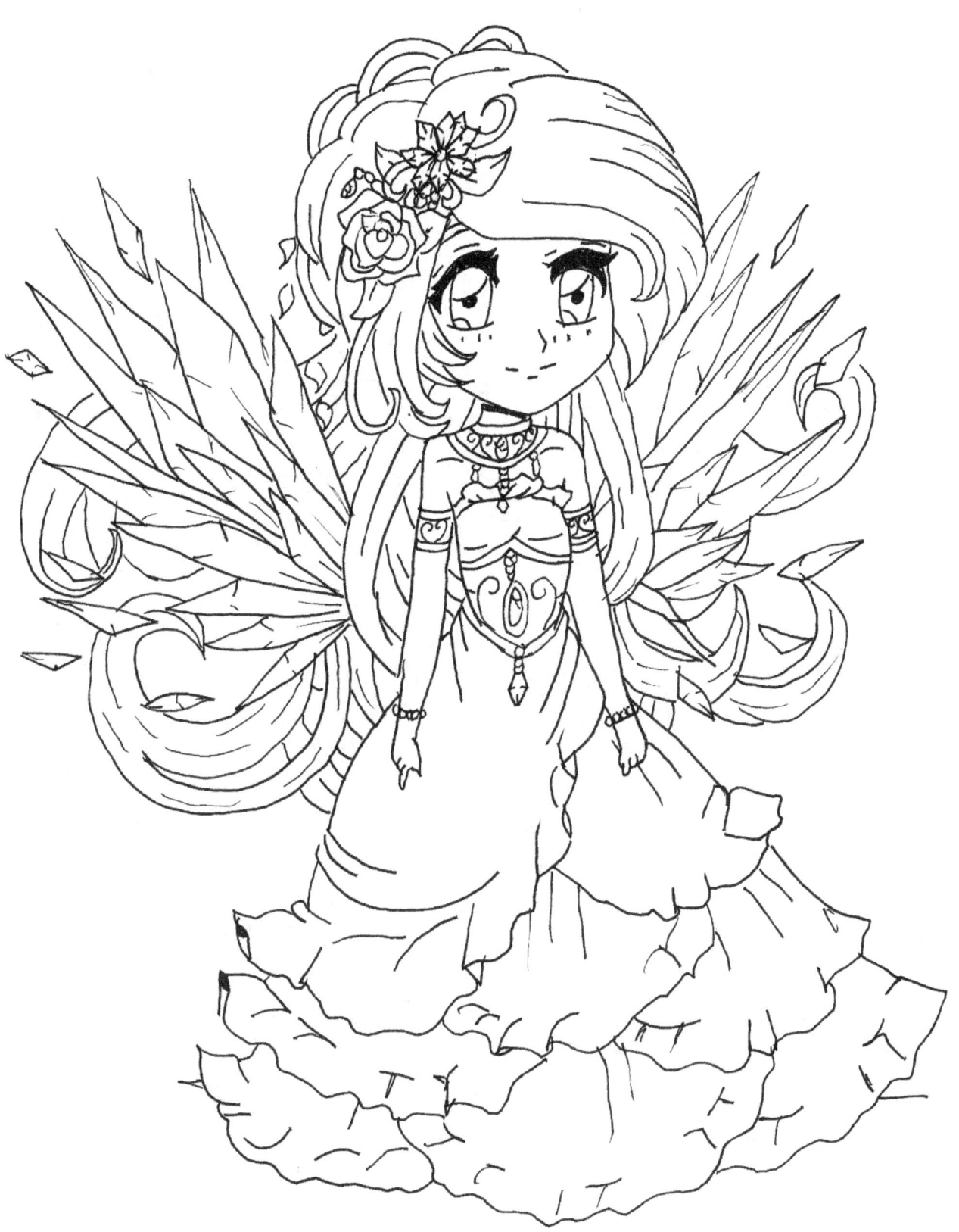

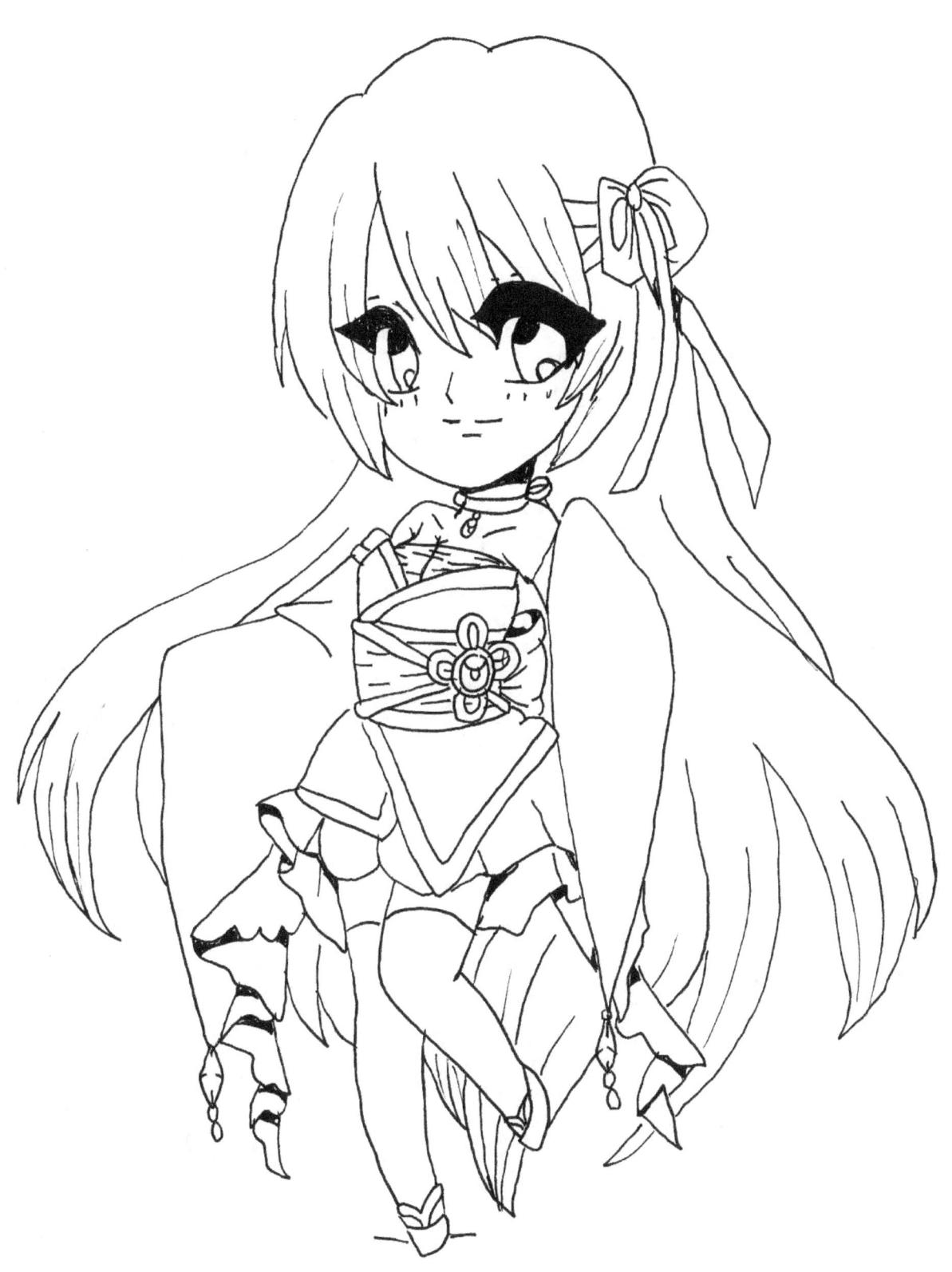

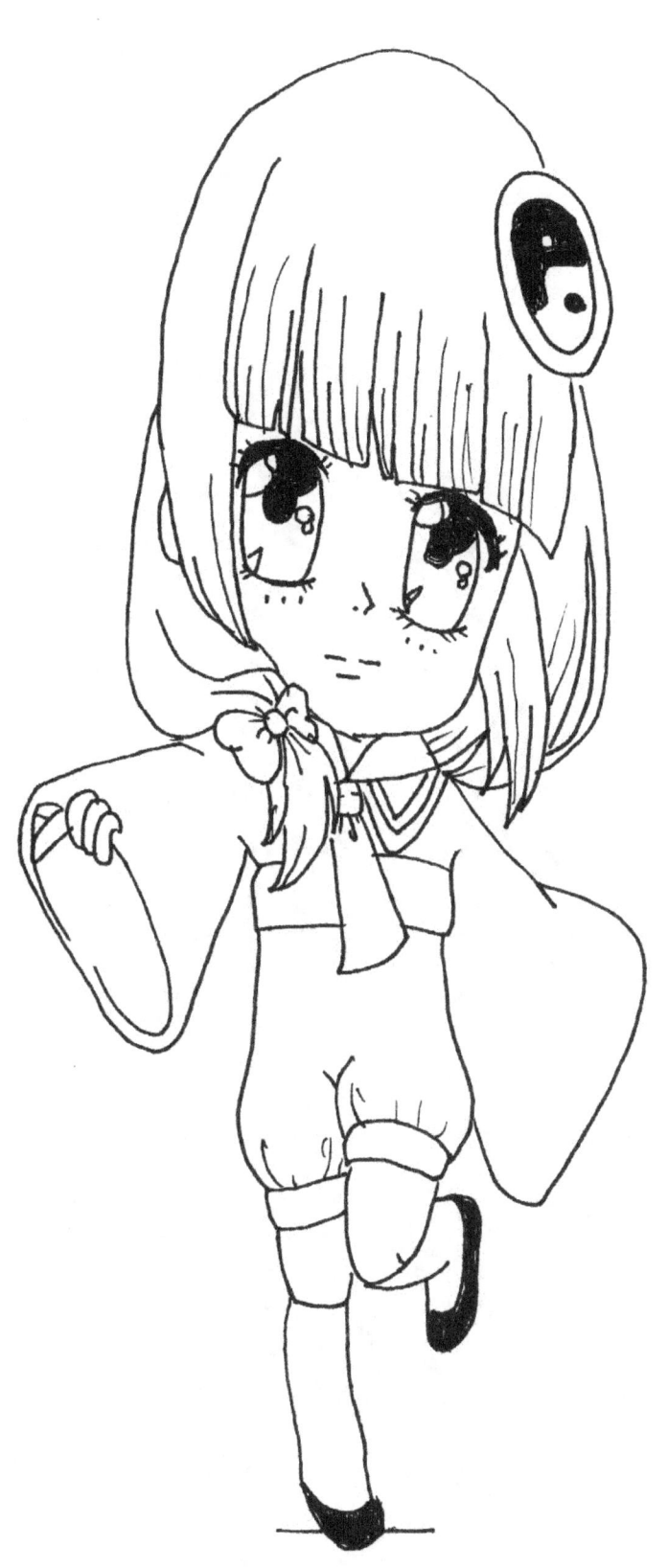

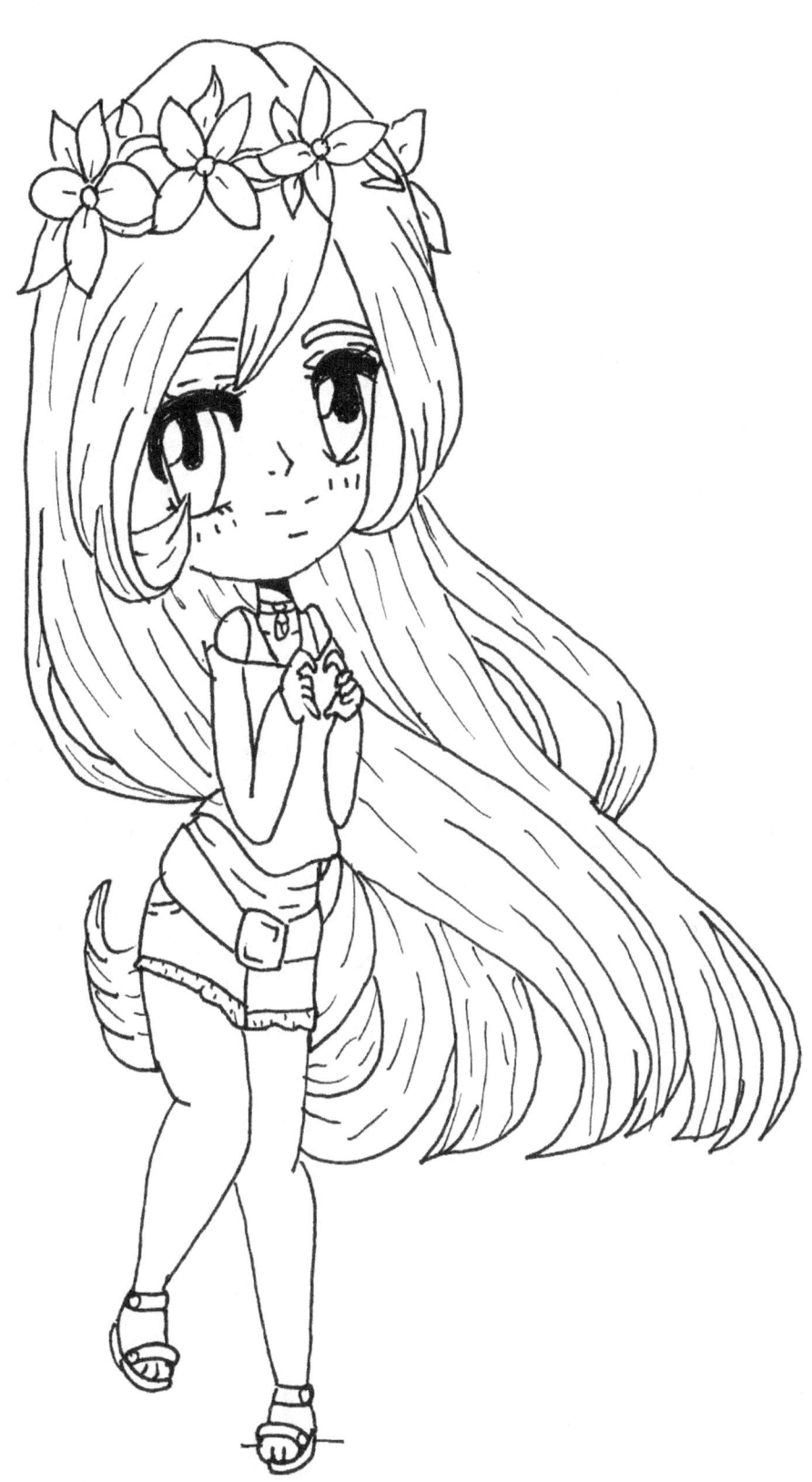

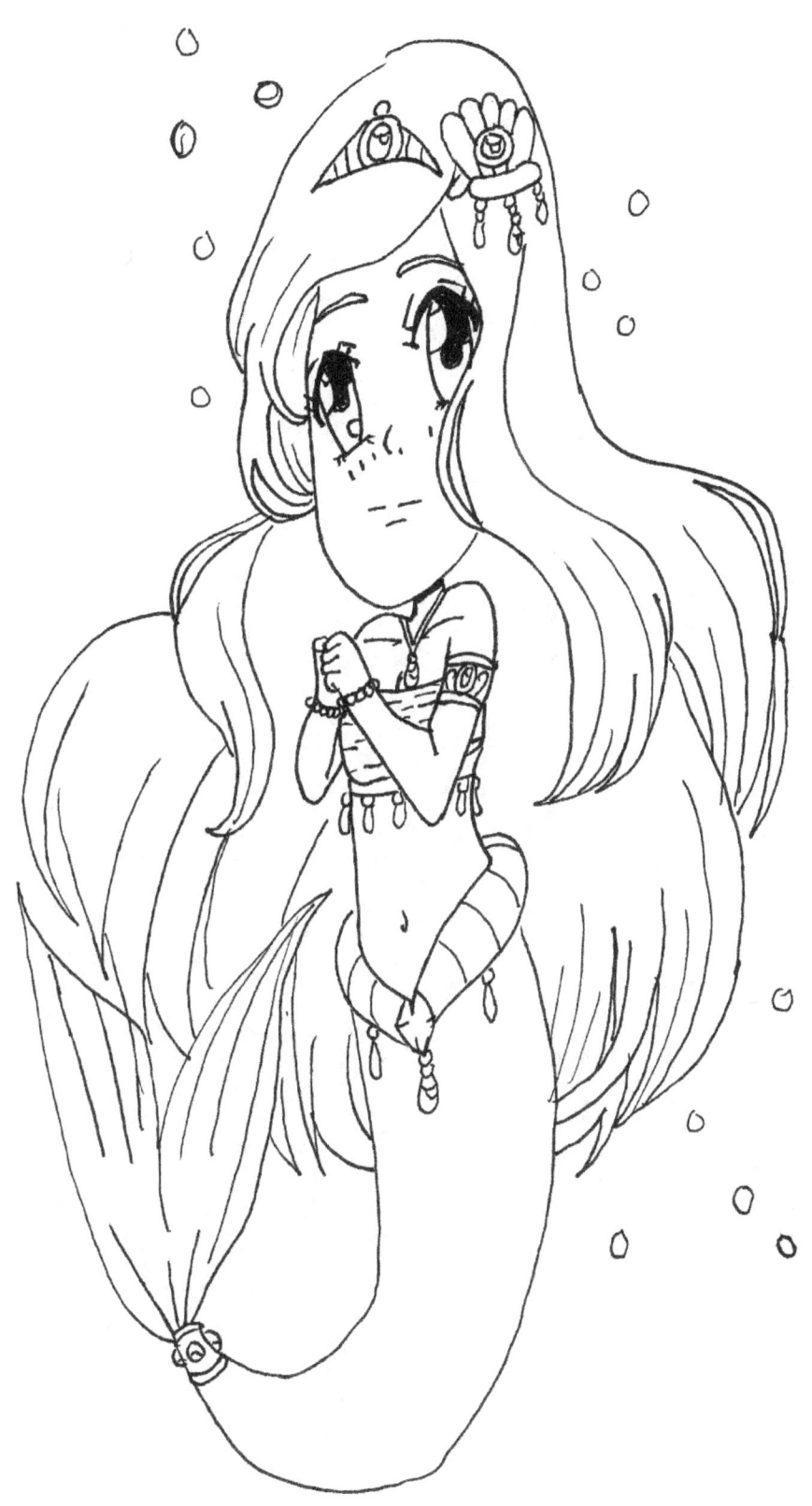

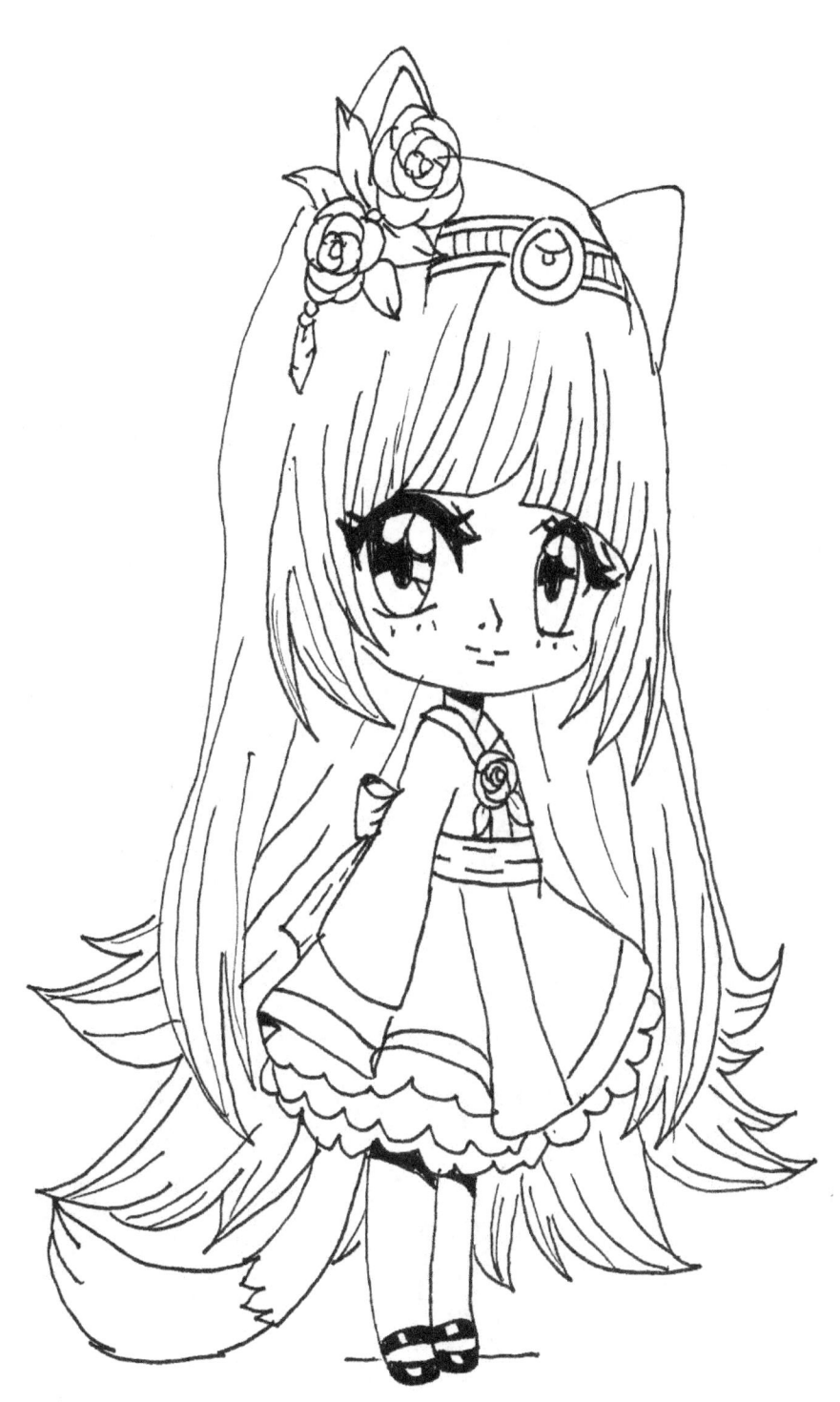

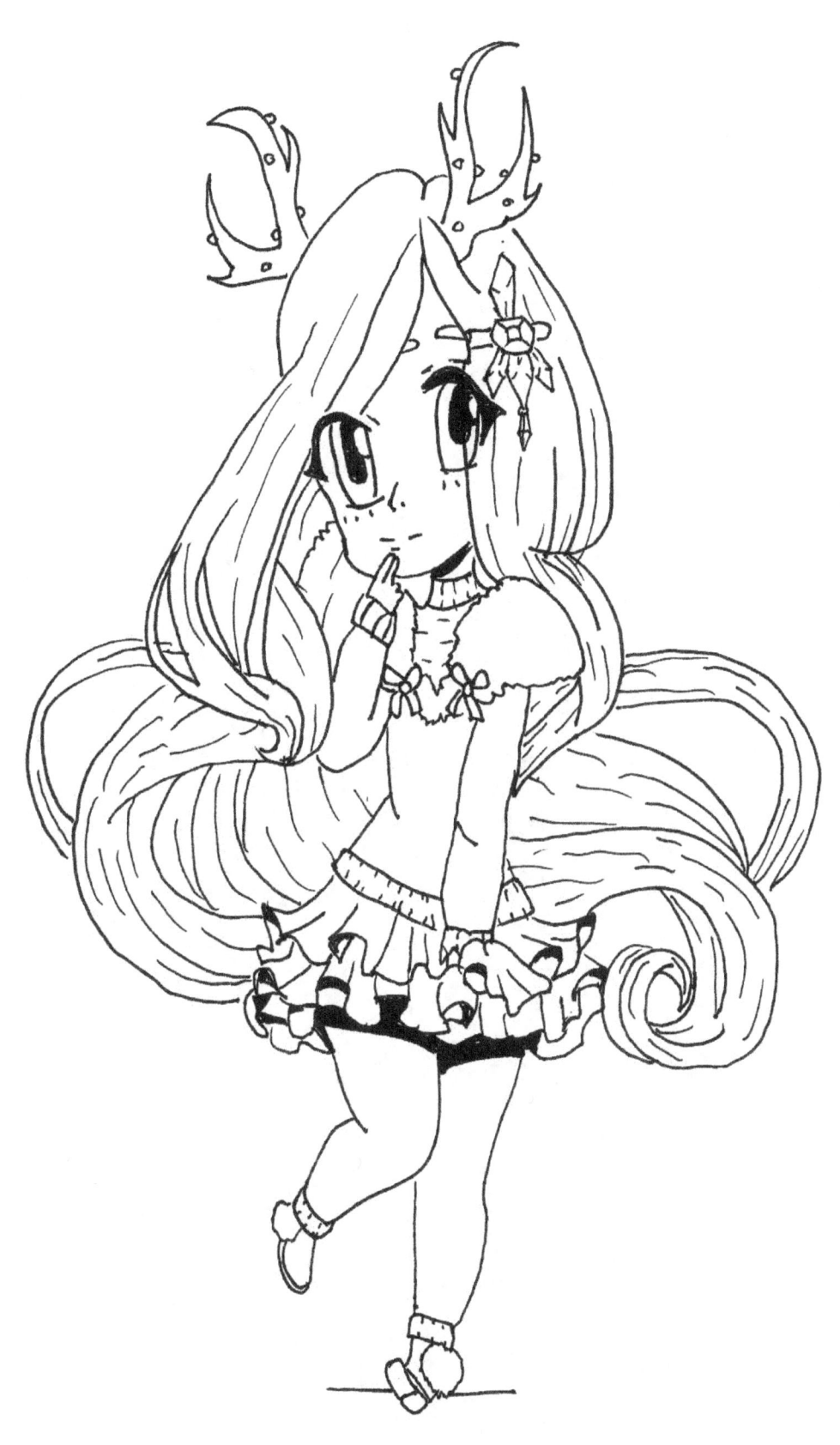

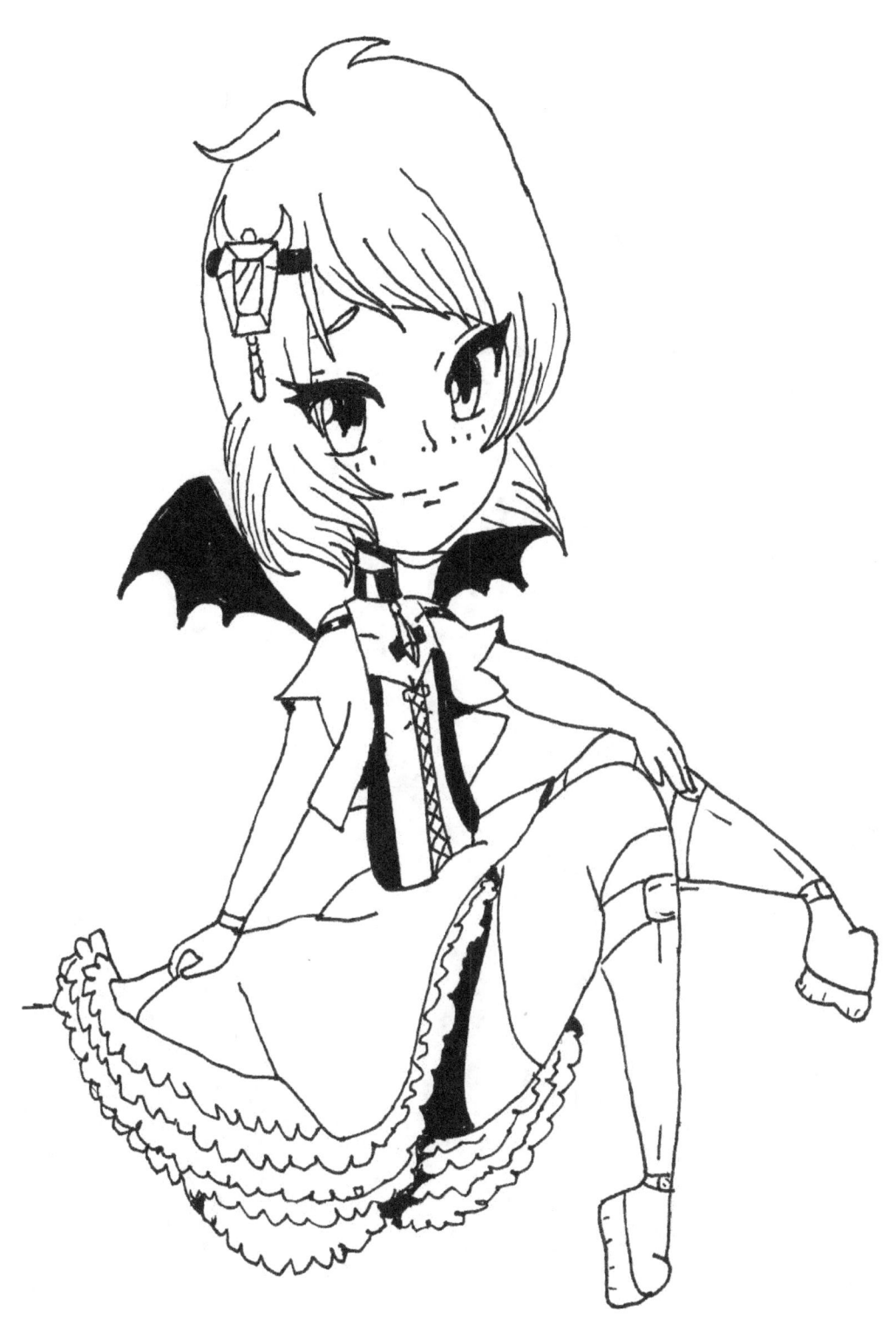

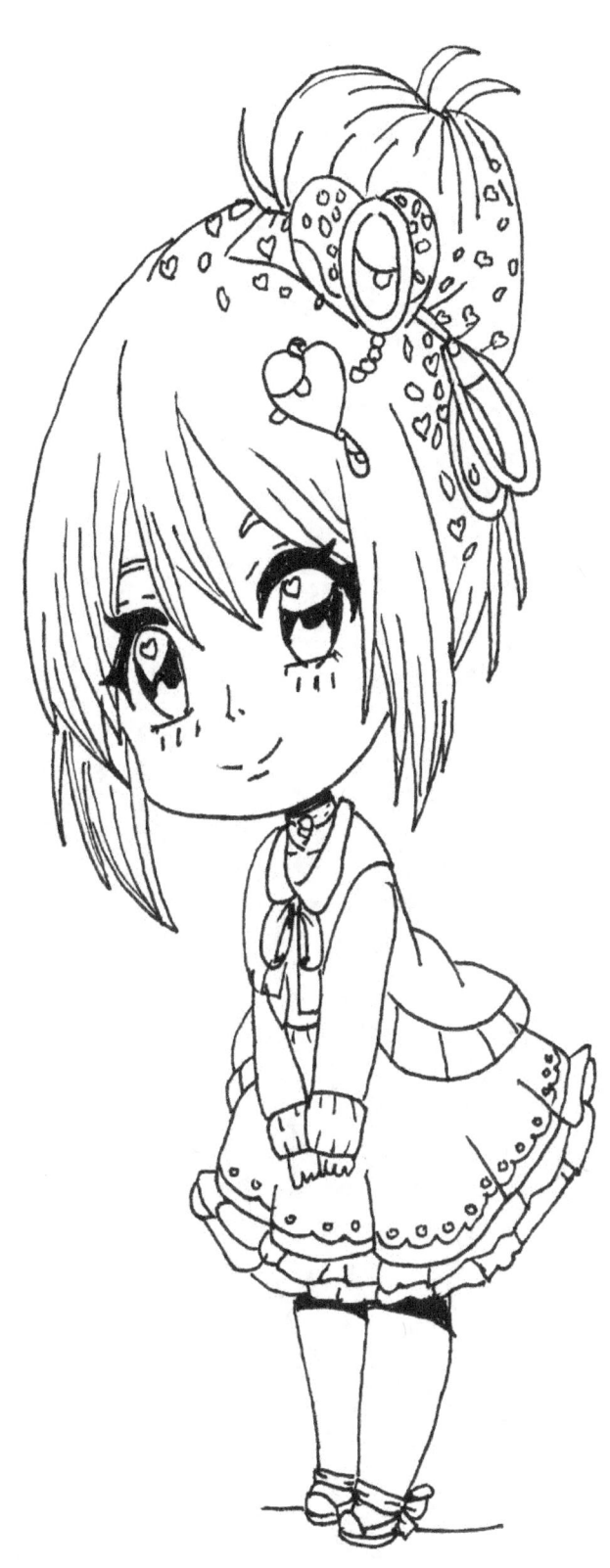

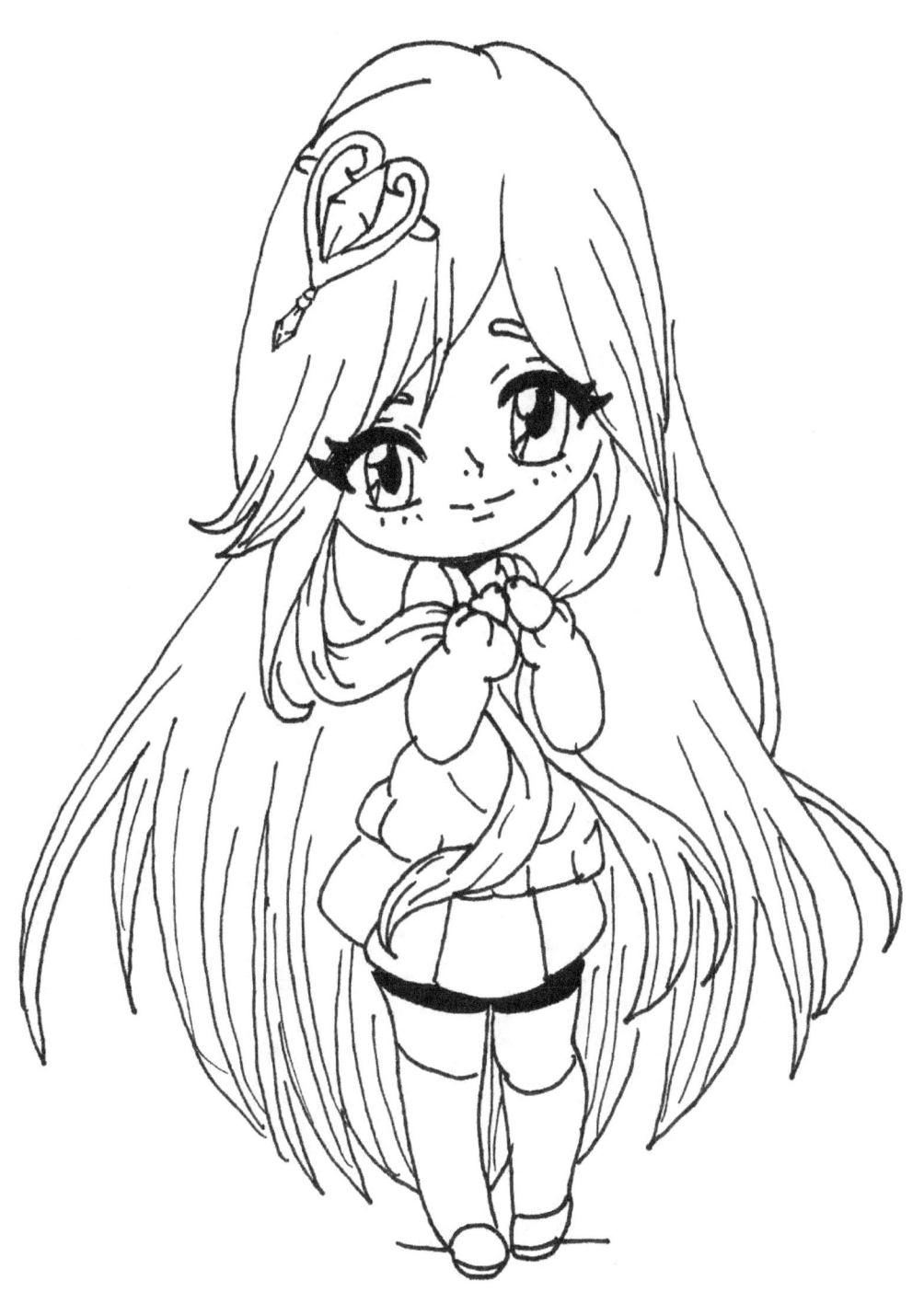

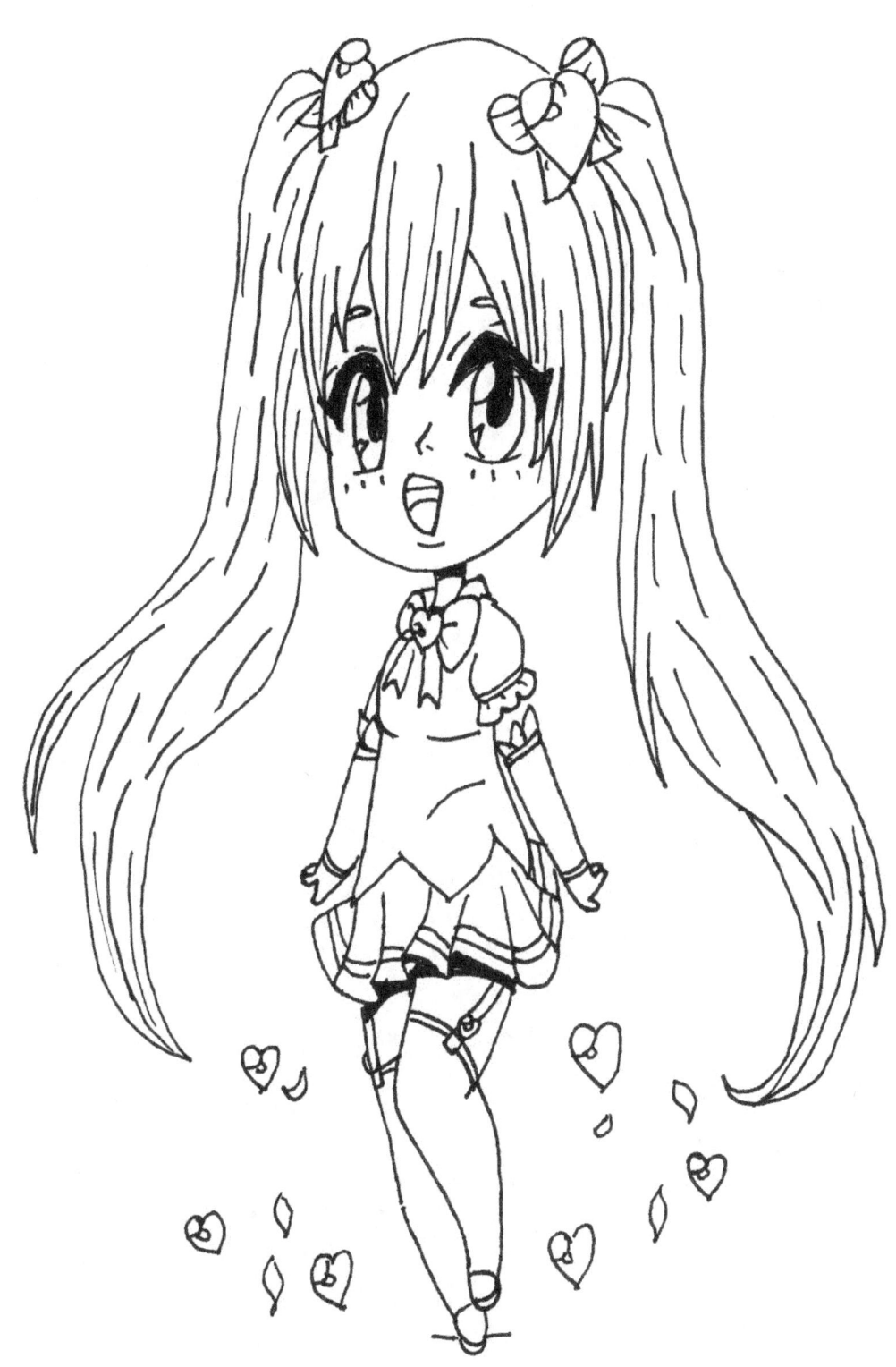

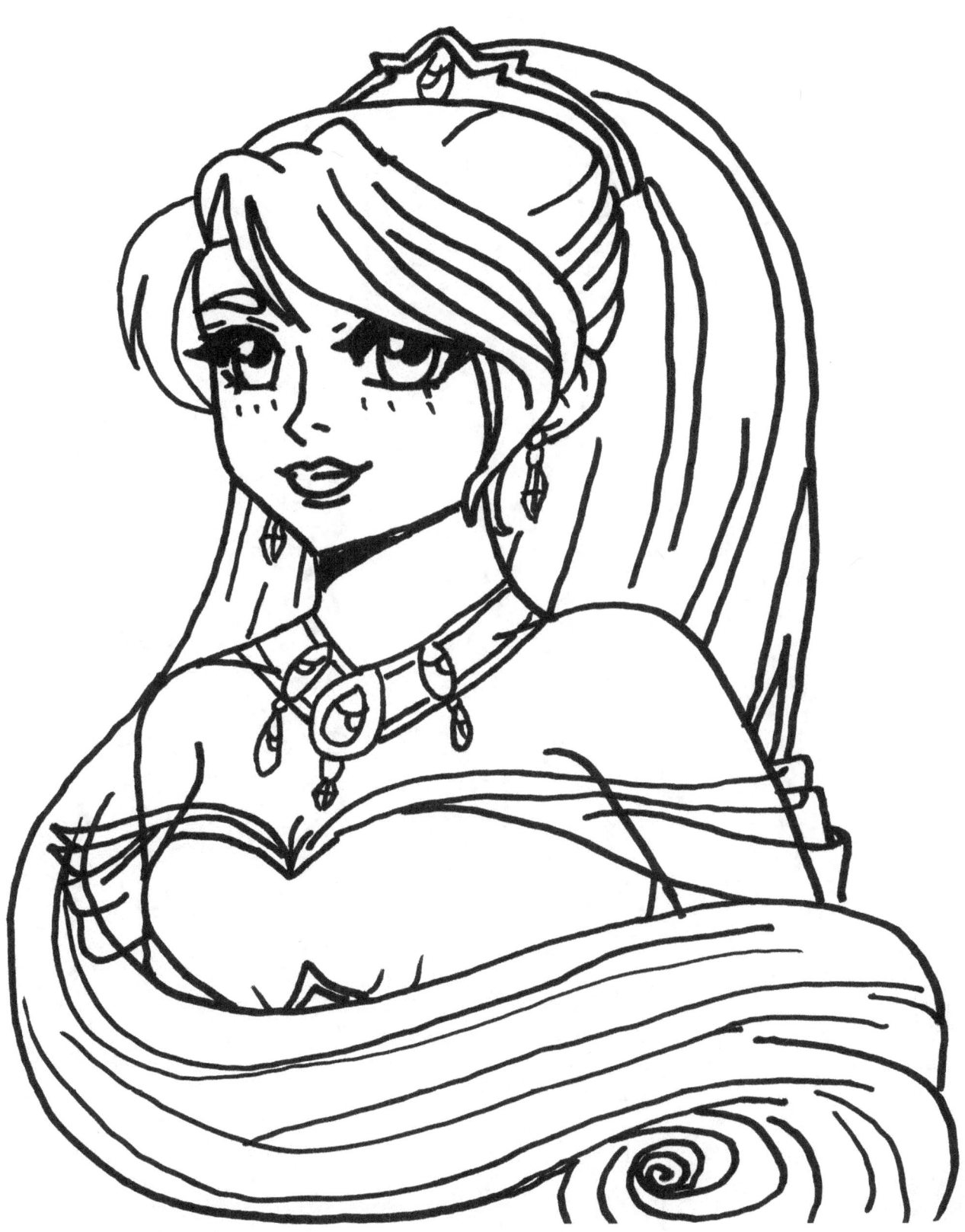

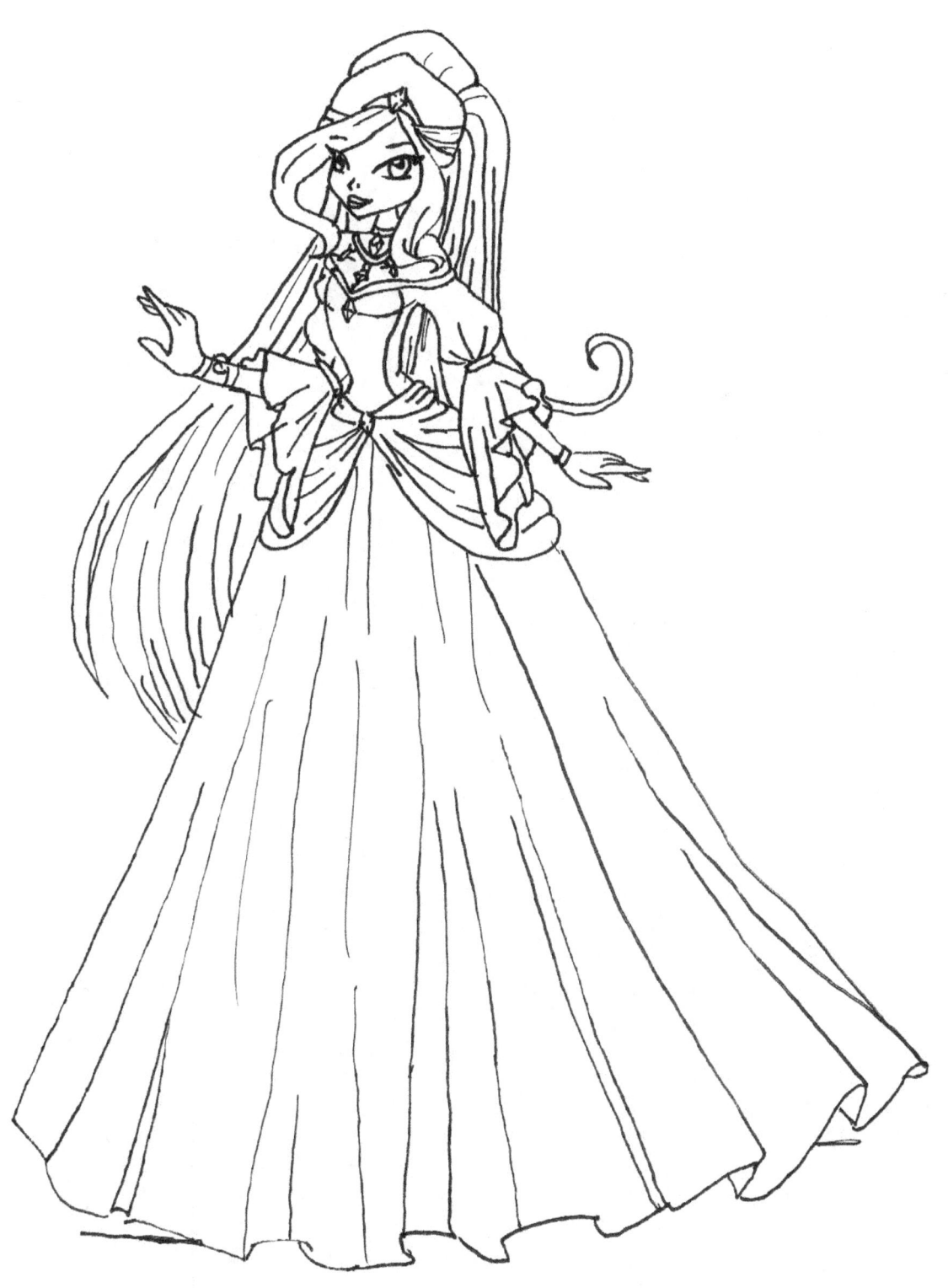

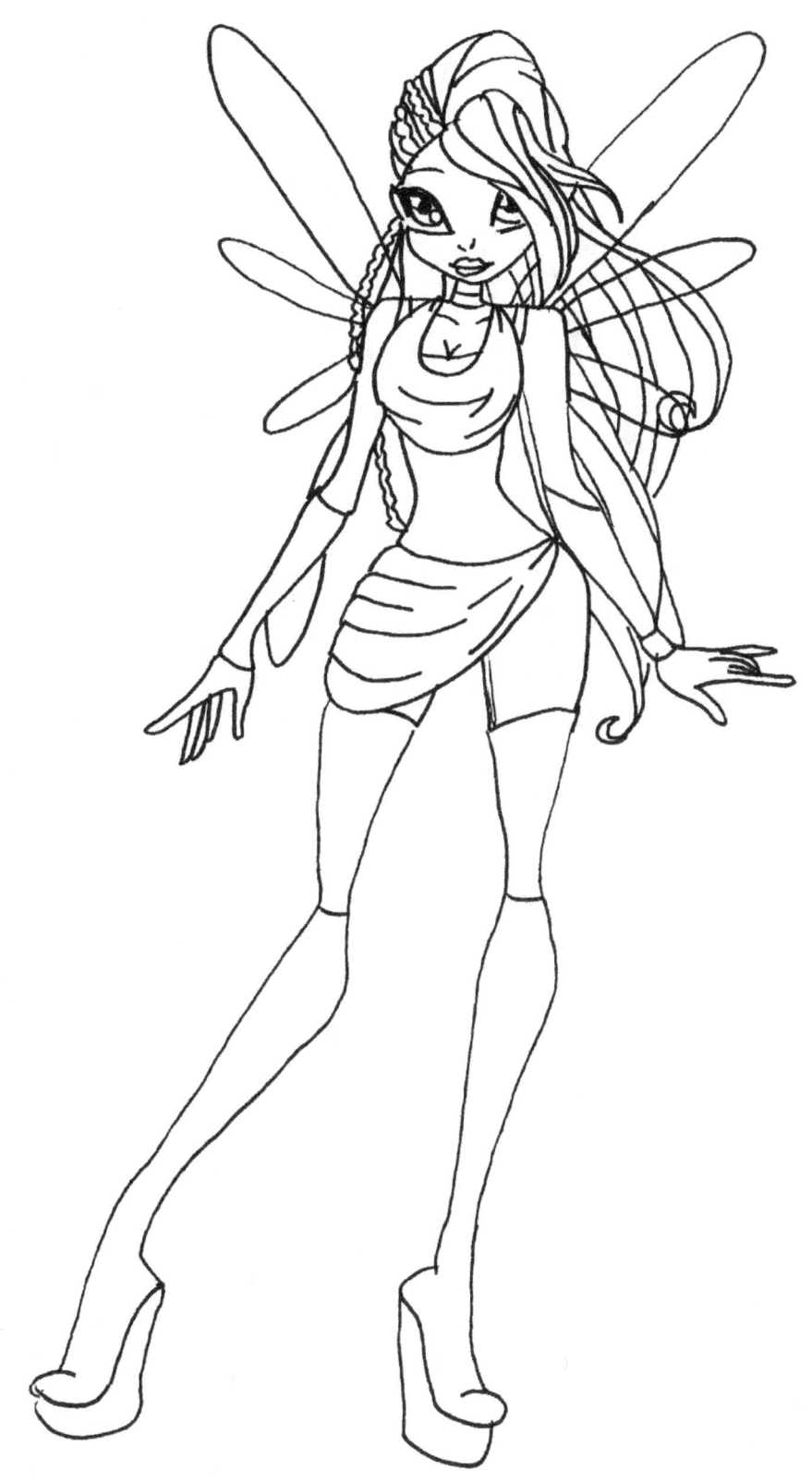

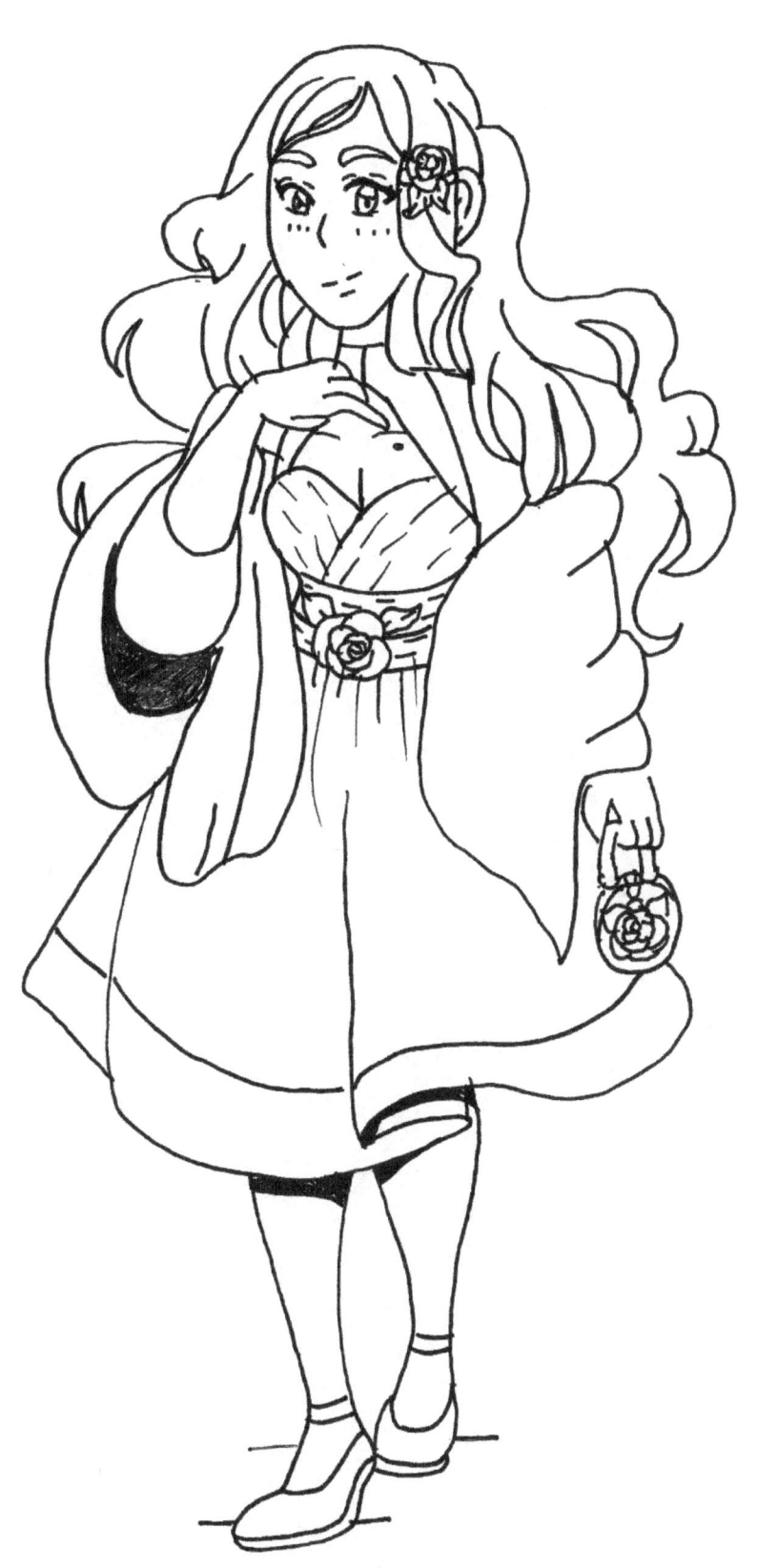

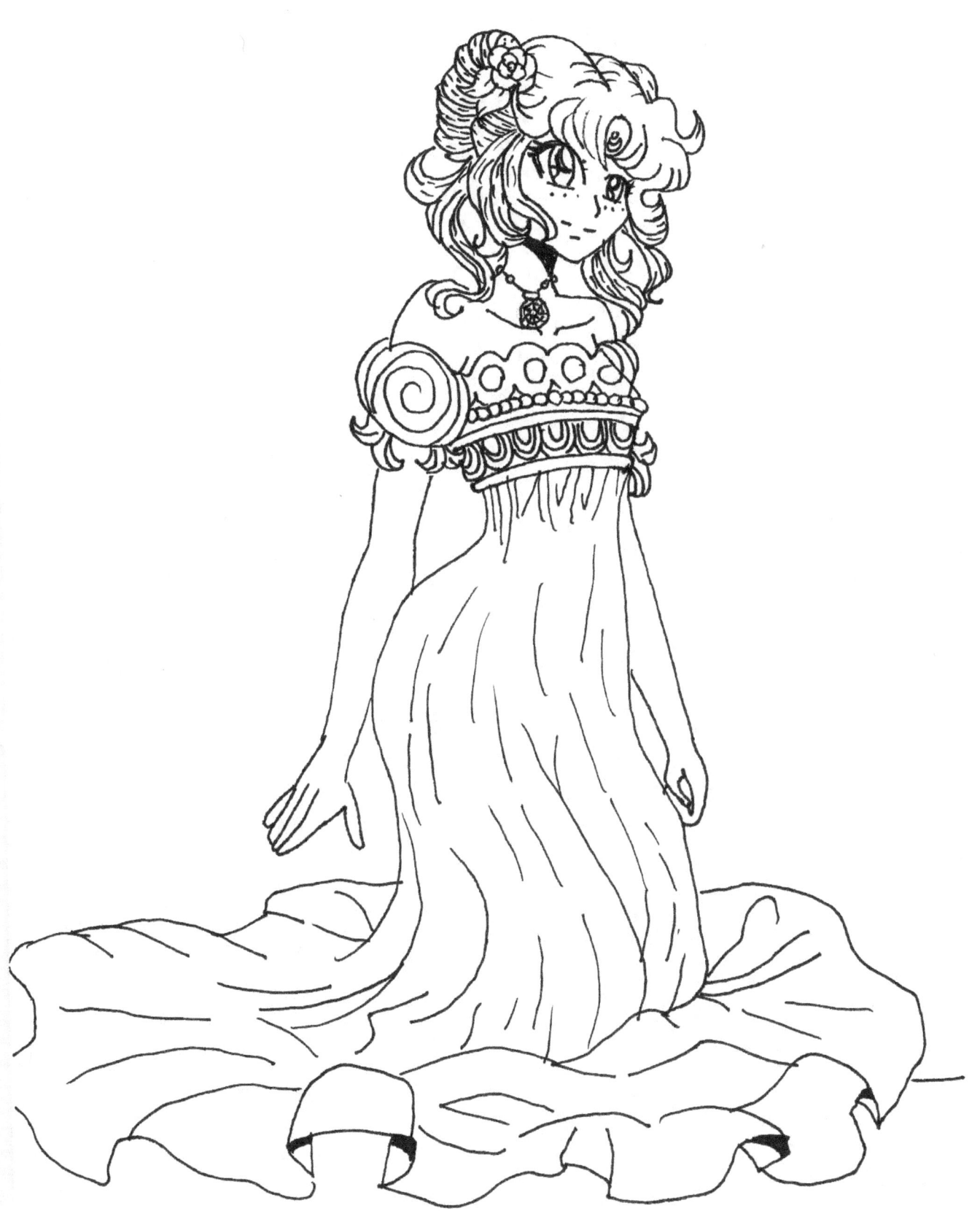

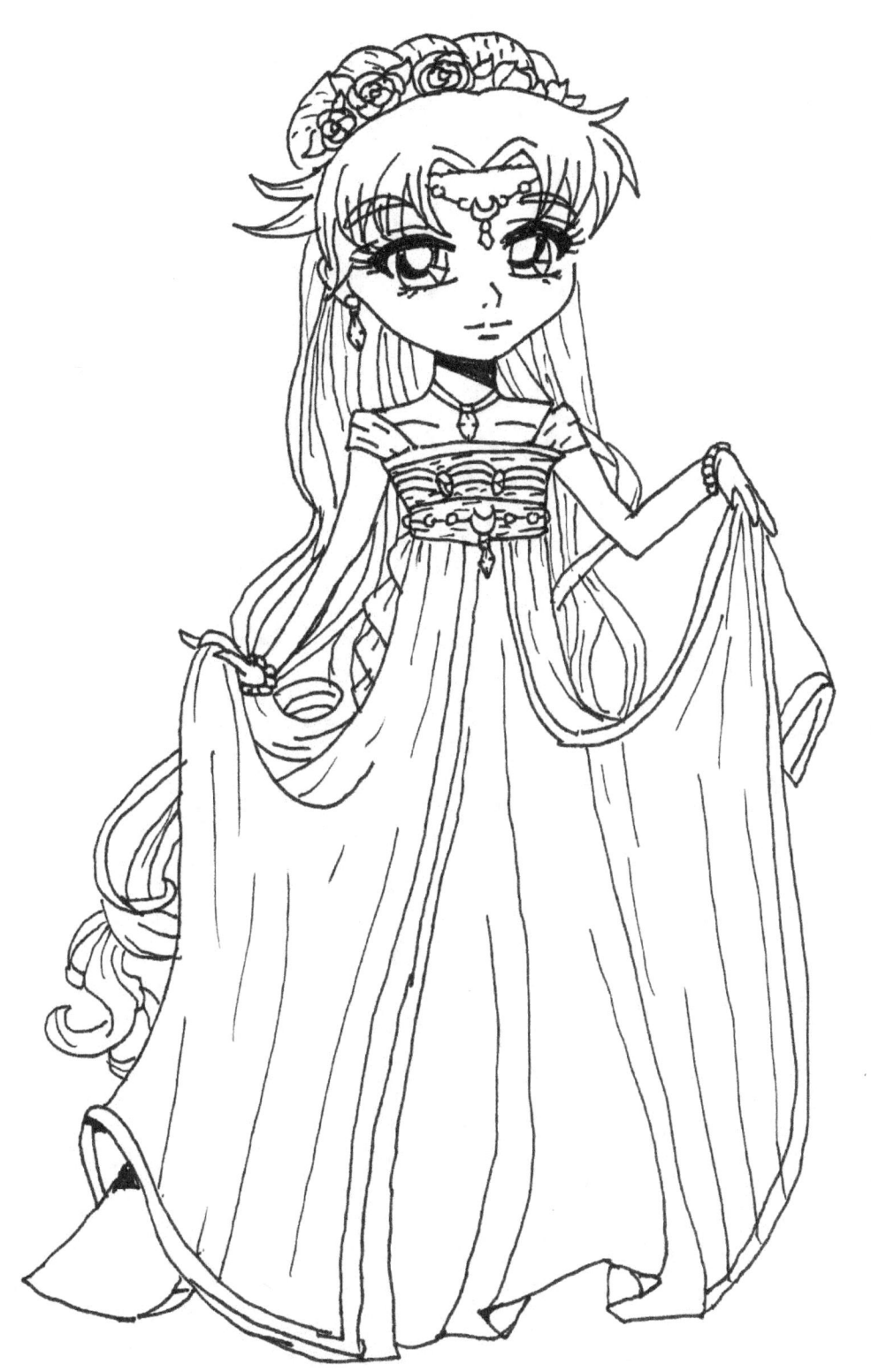

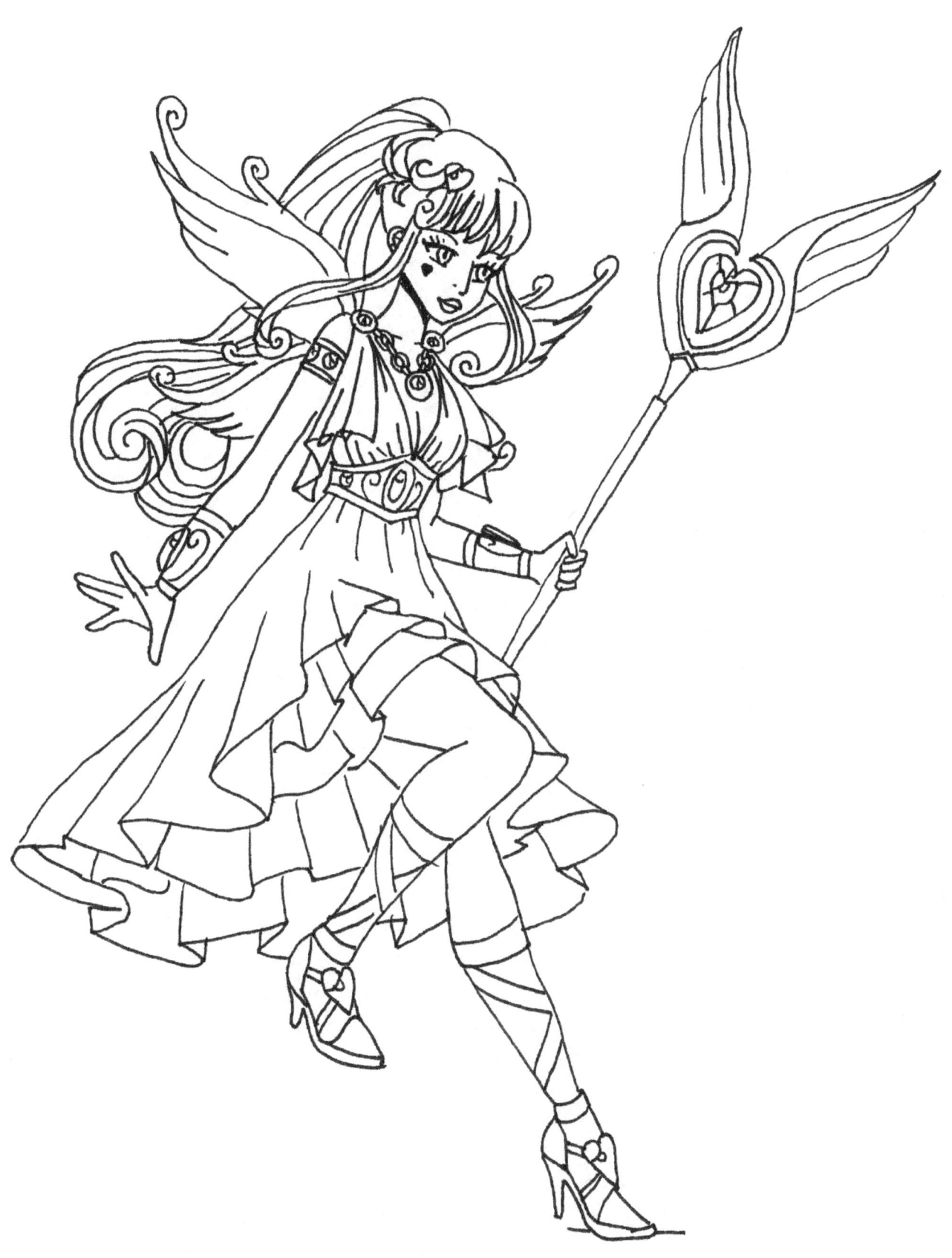

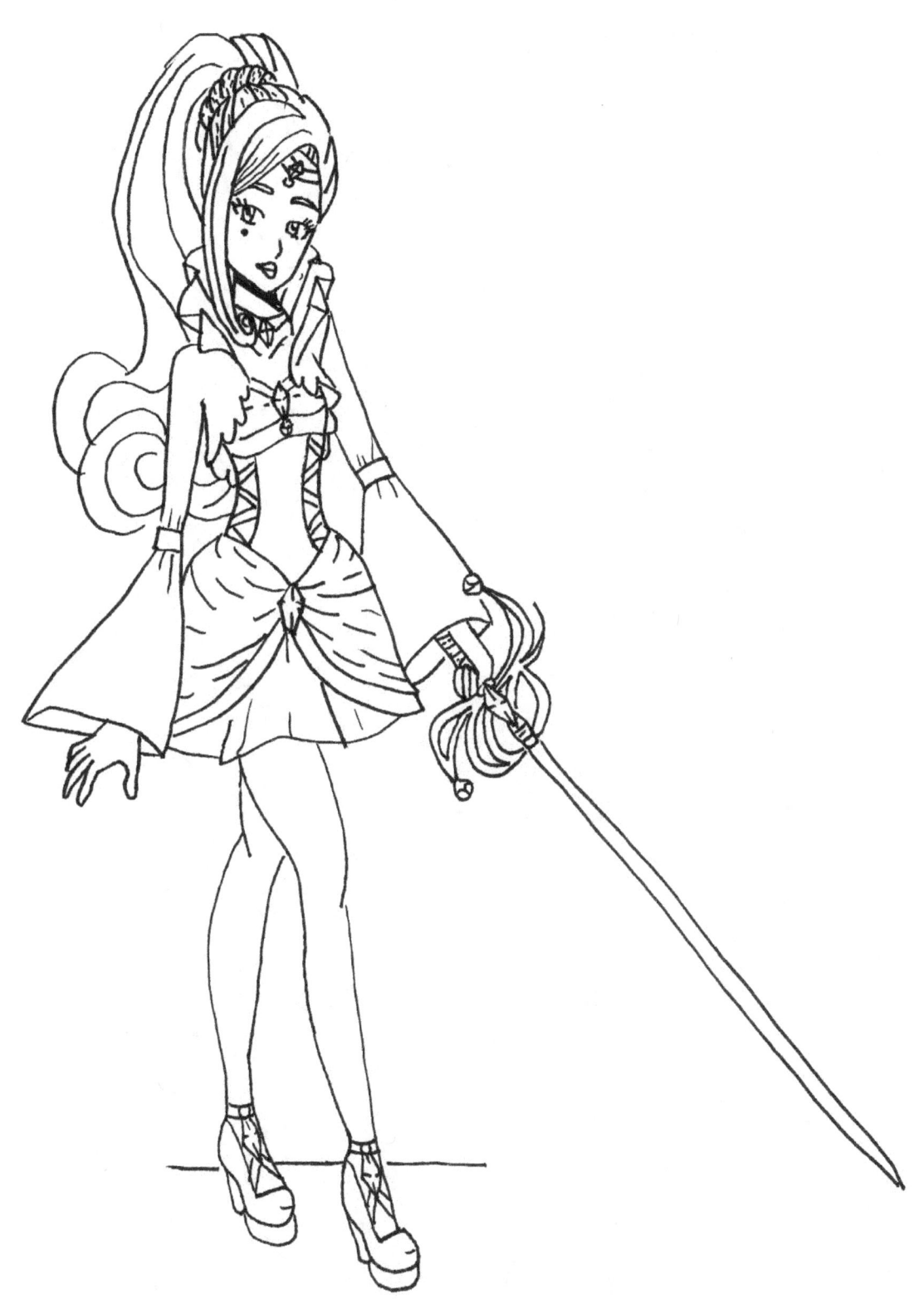

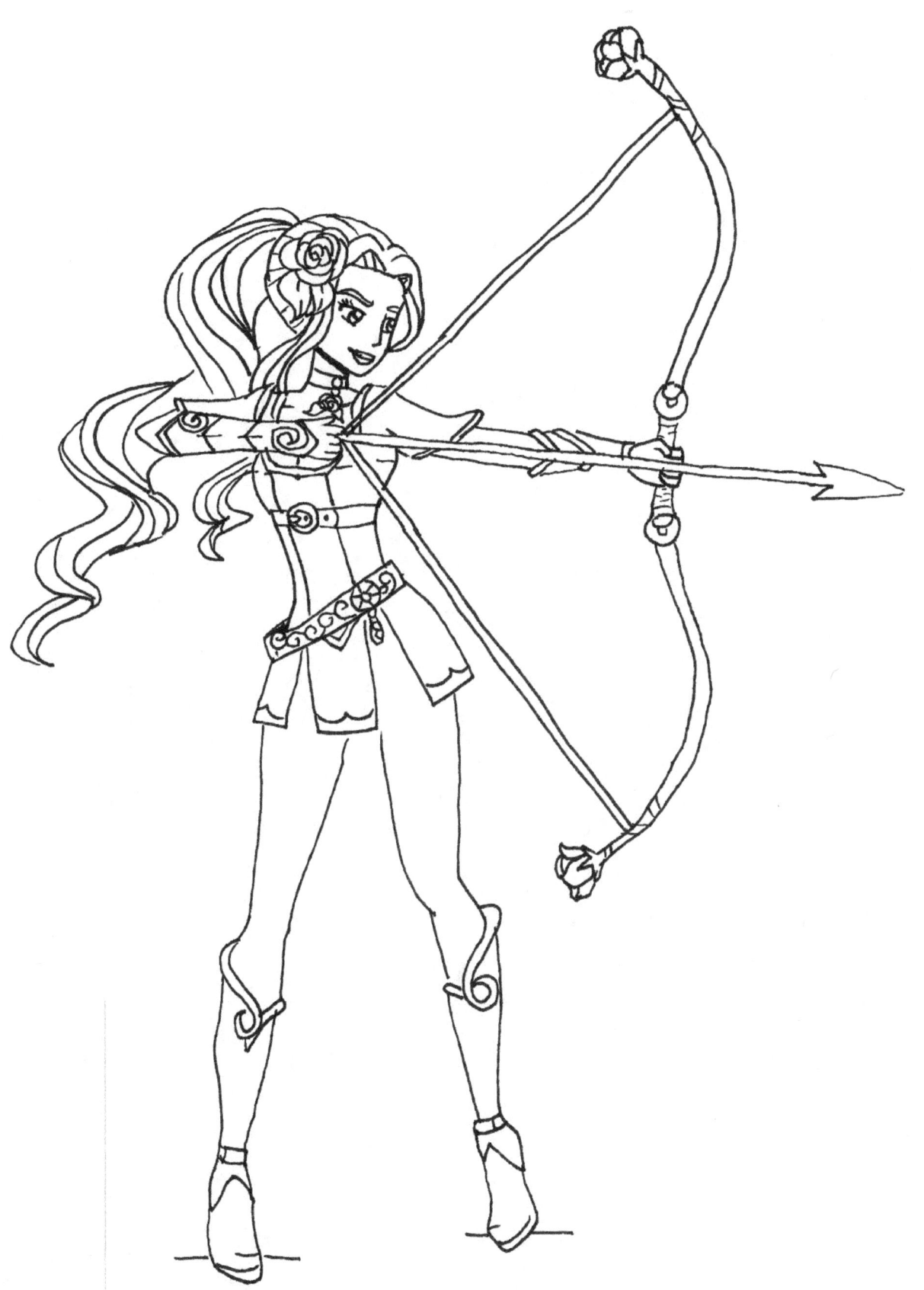

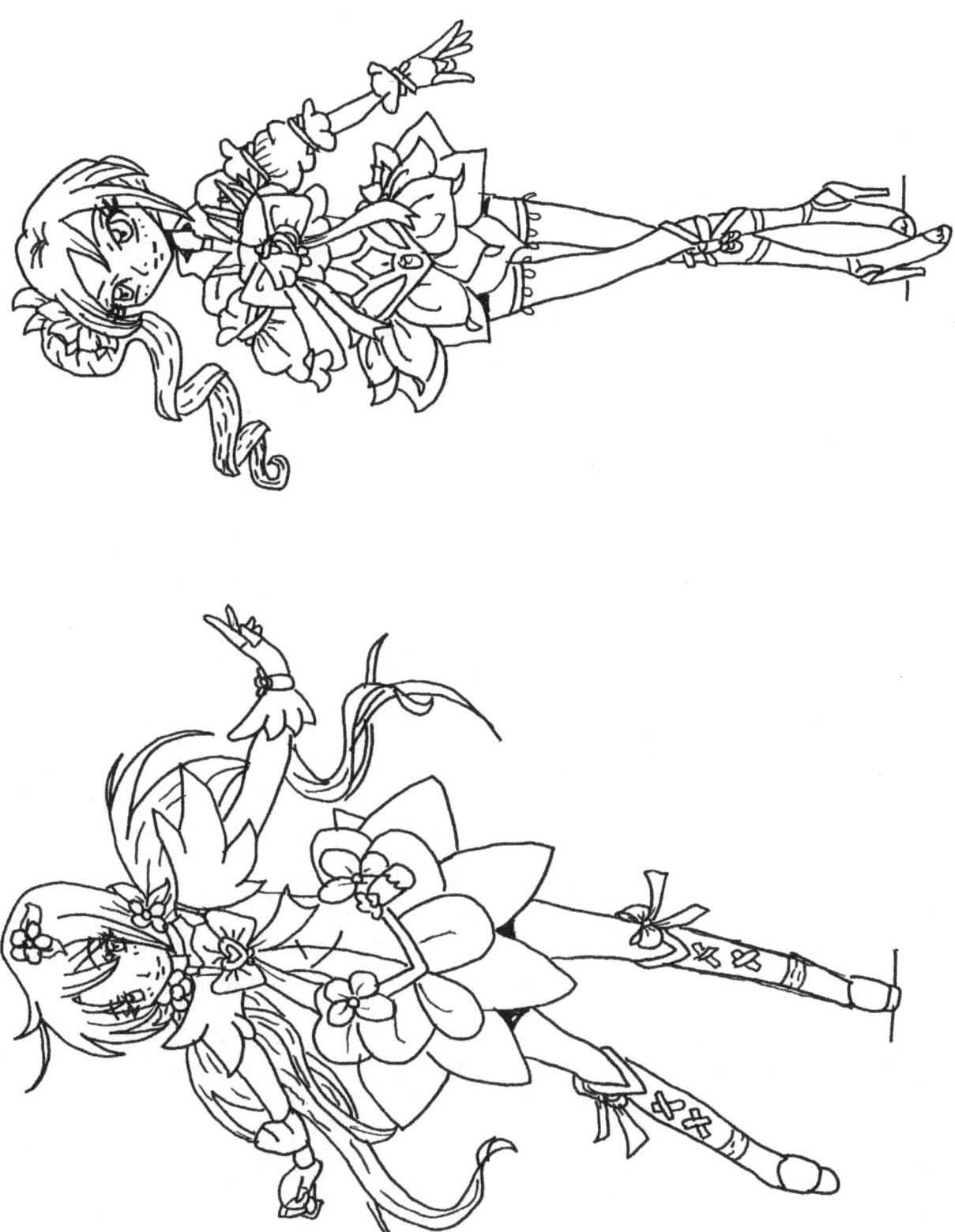

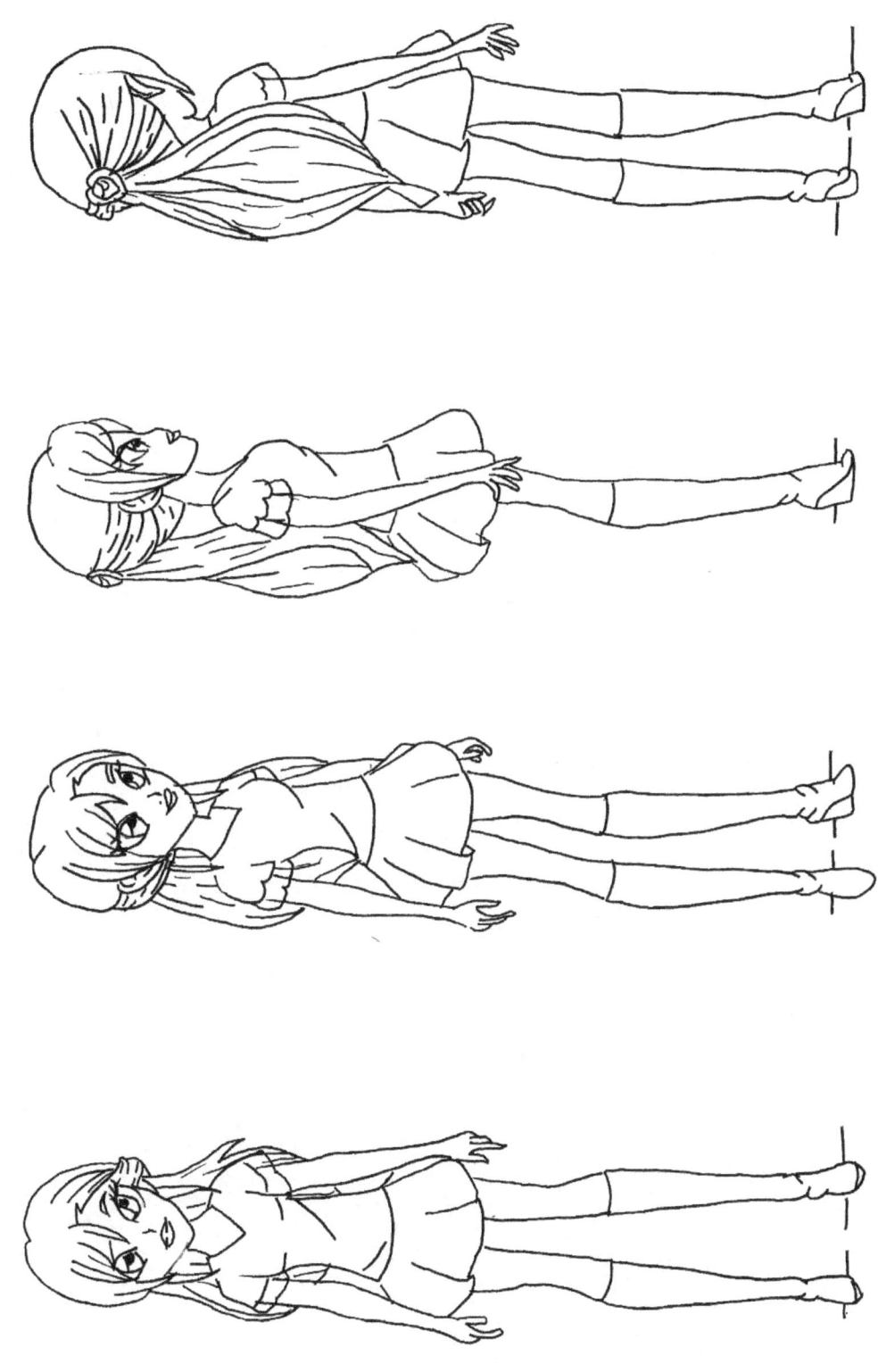

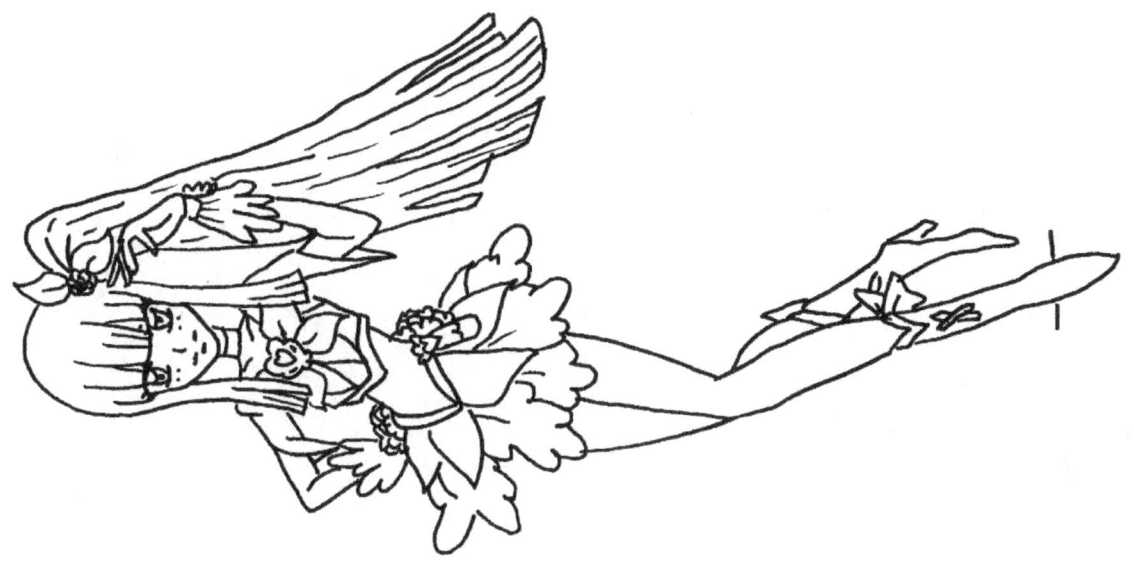
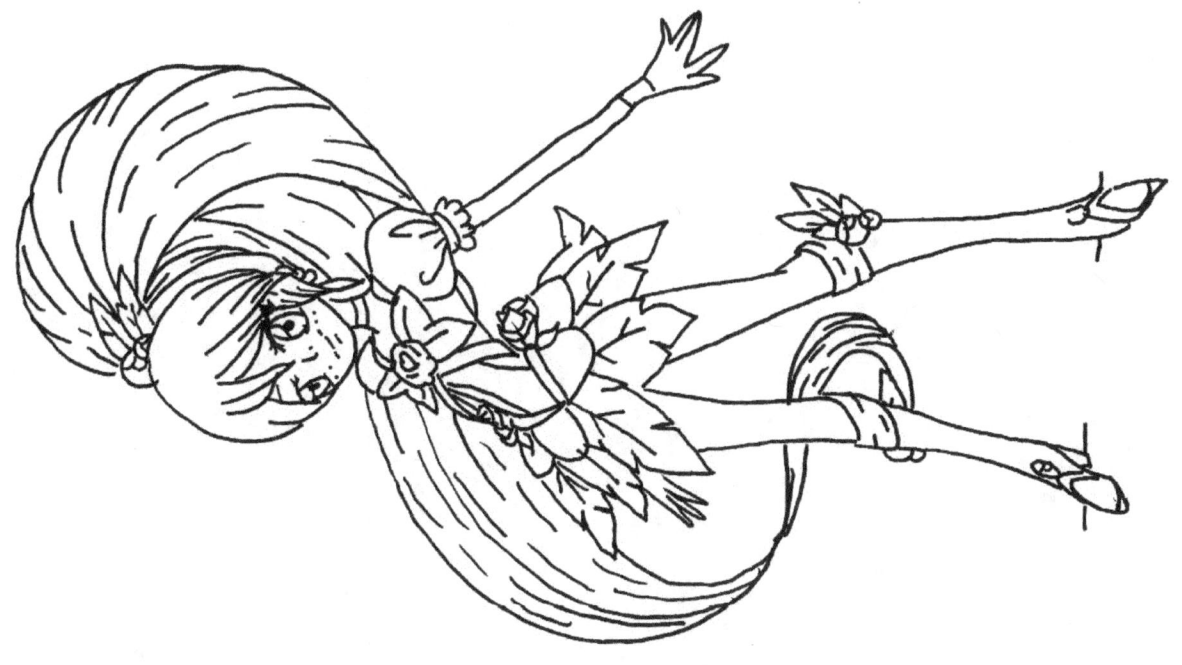

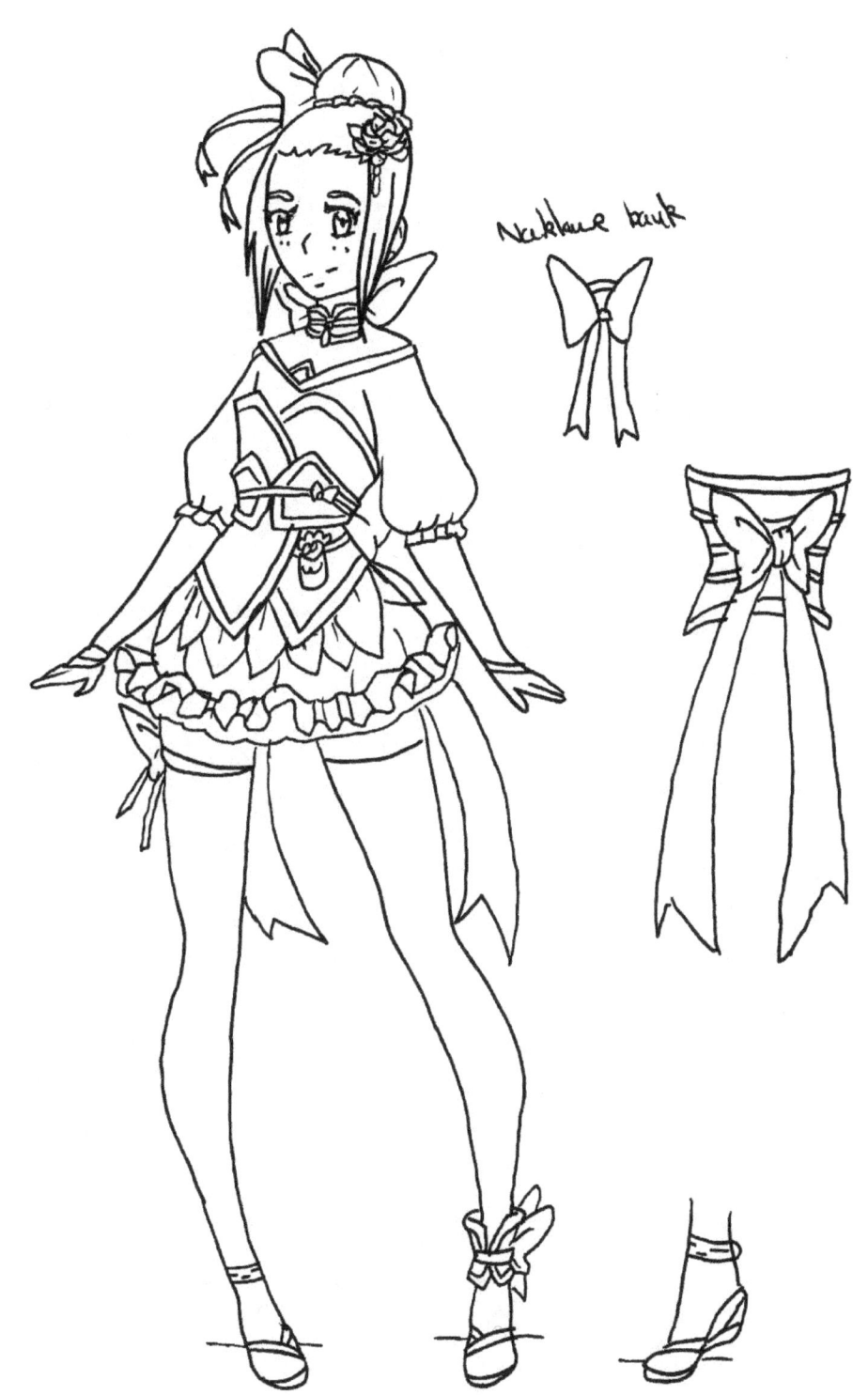

Necklace back

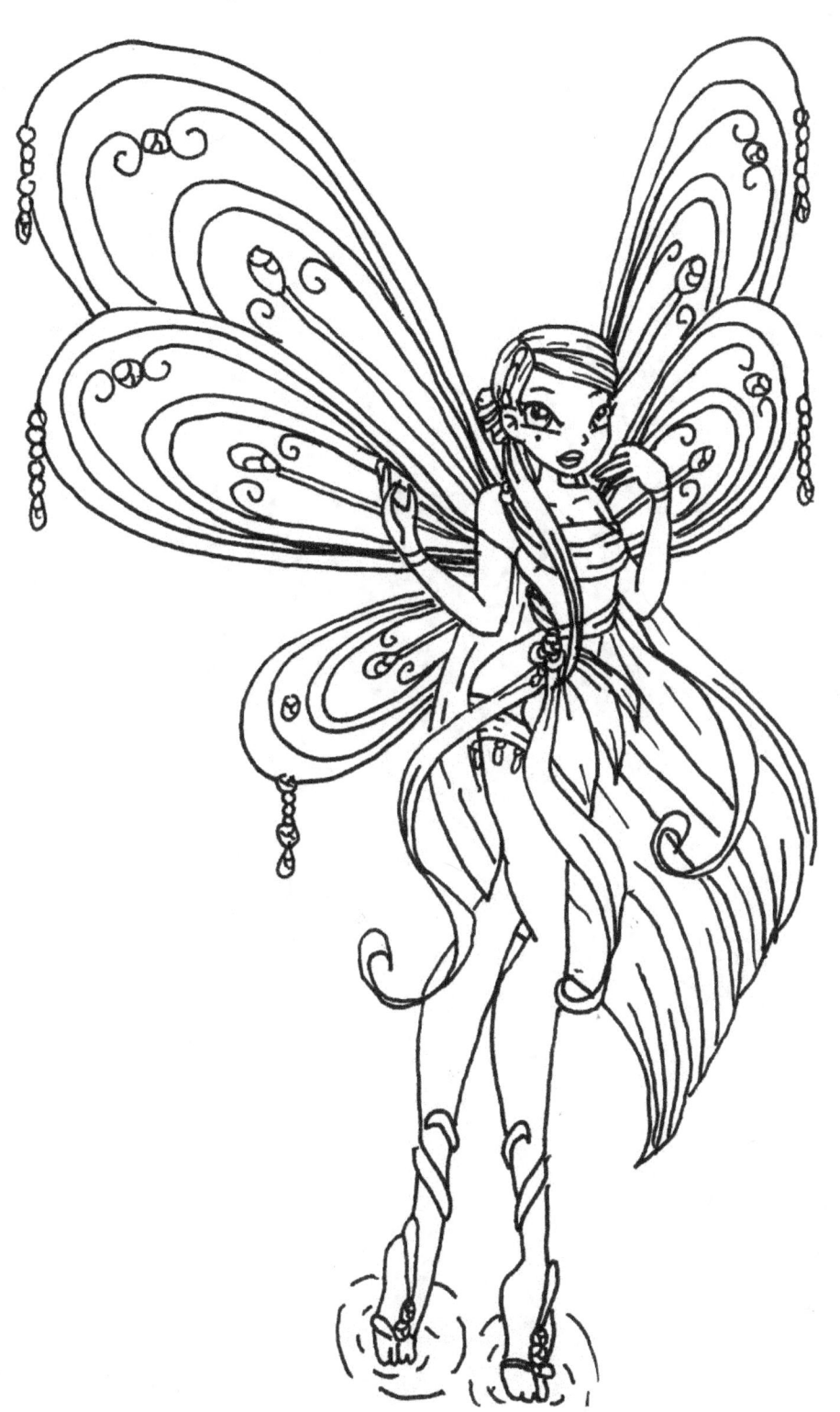

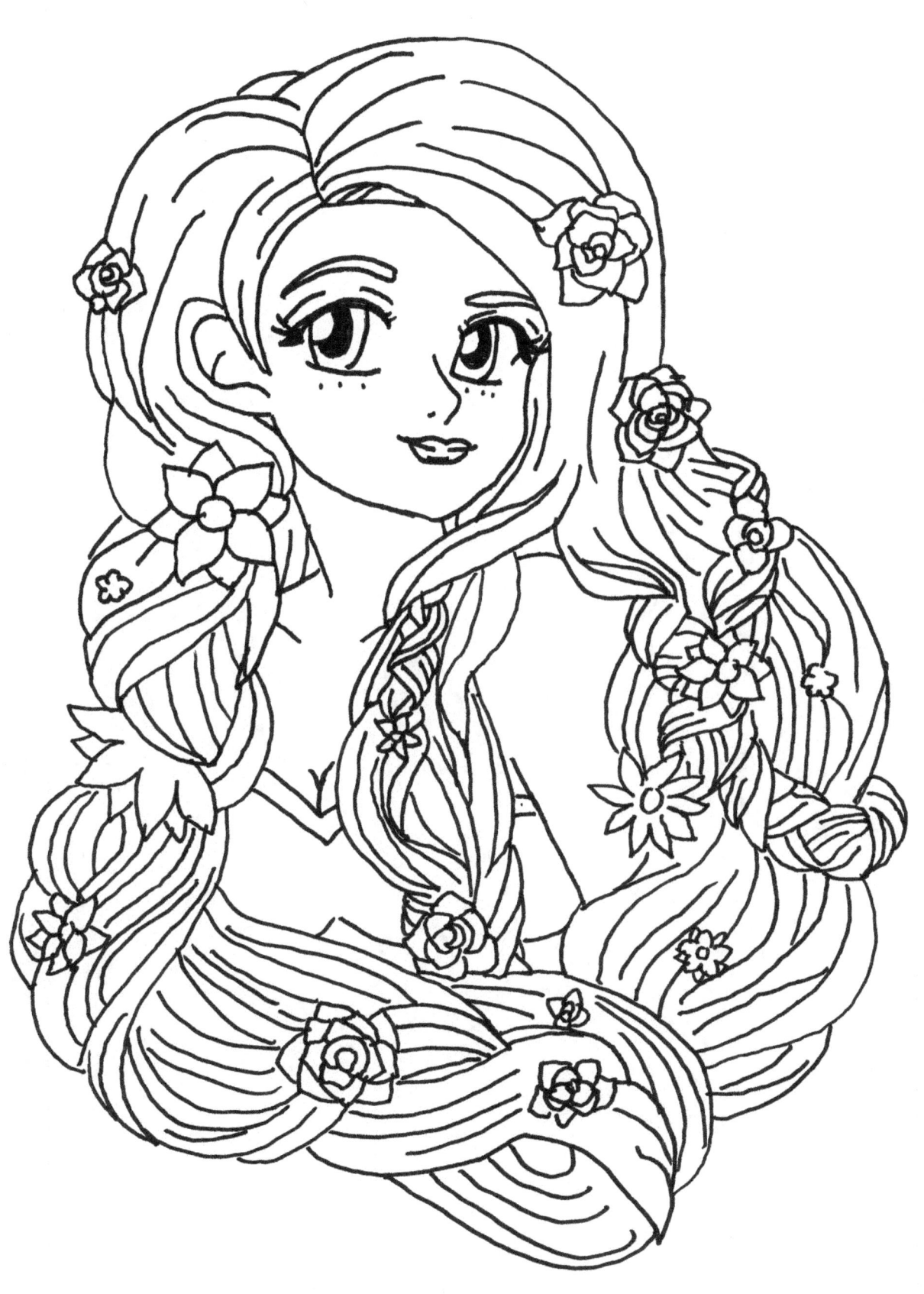

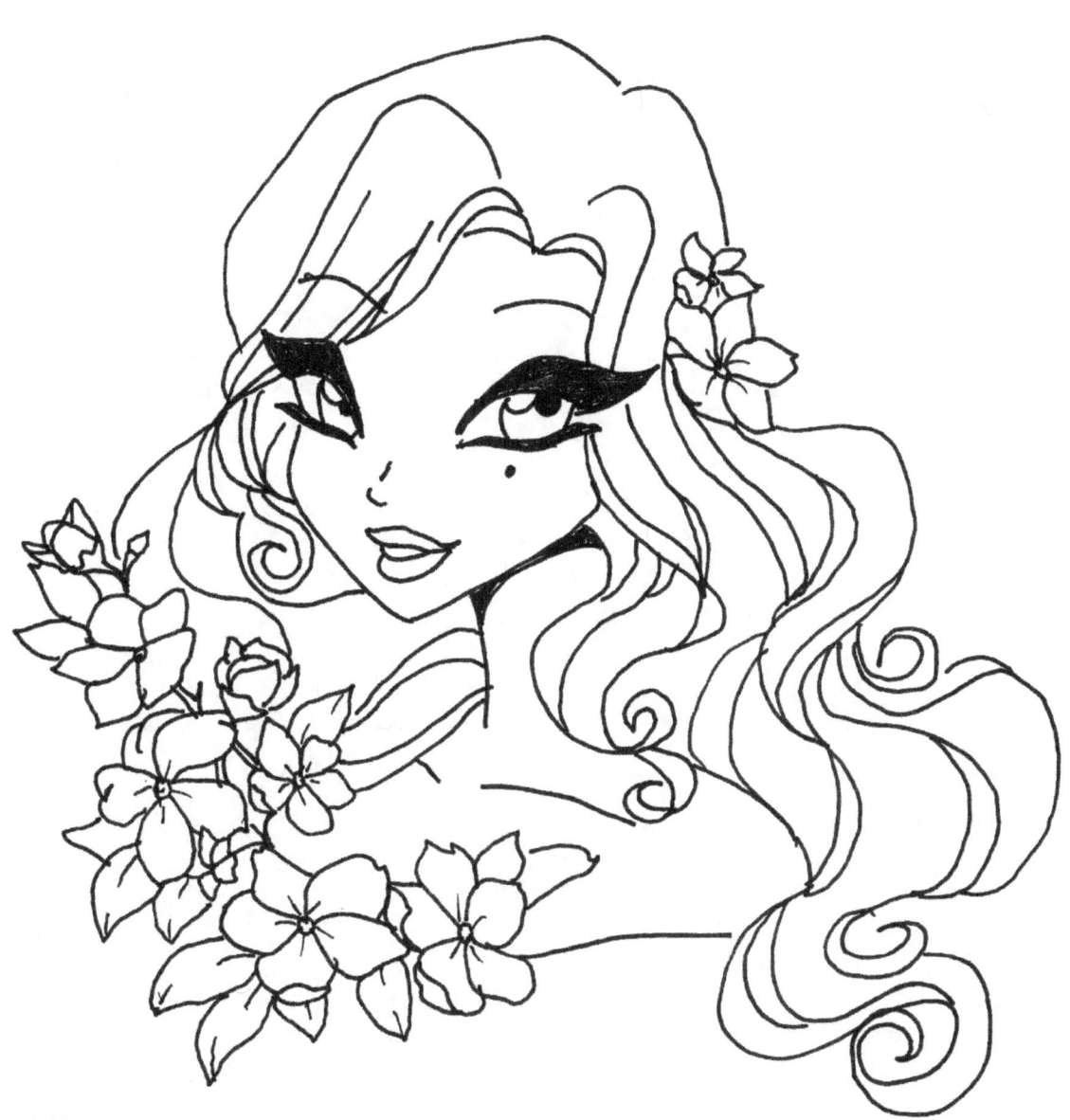

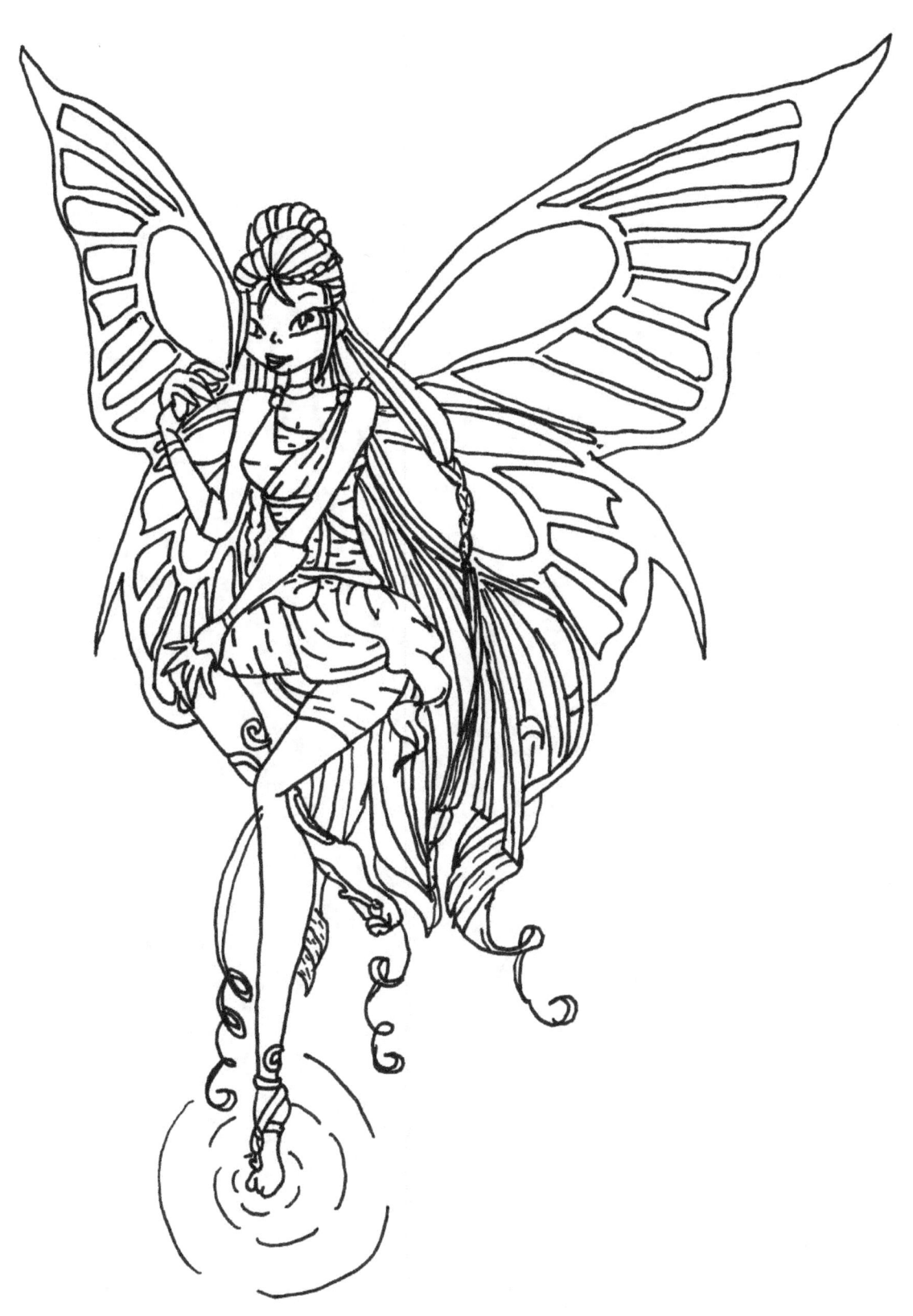

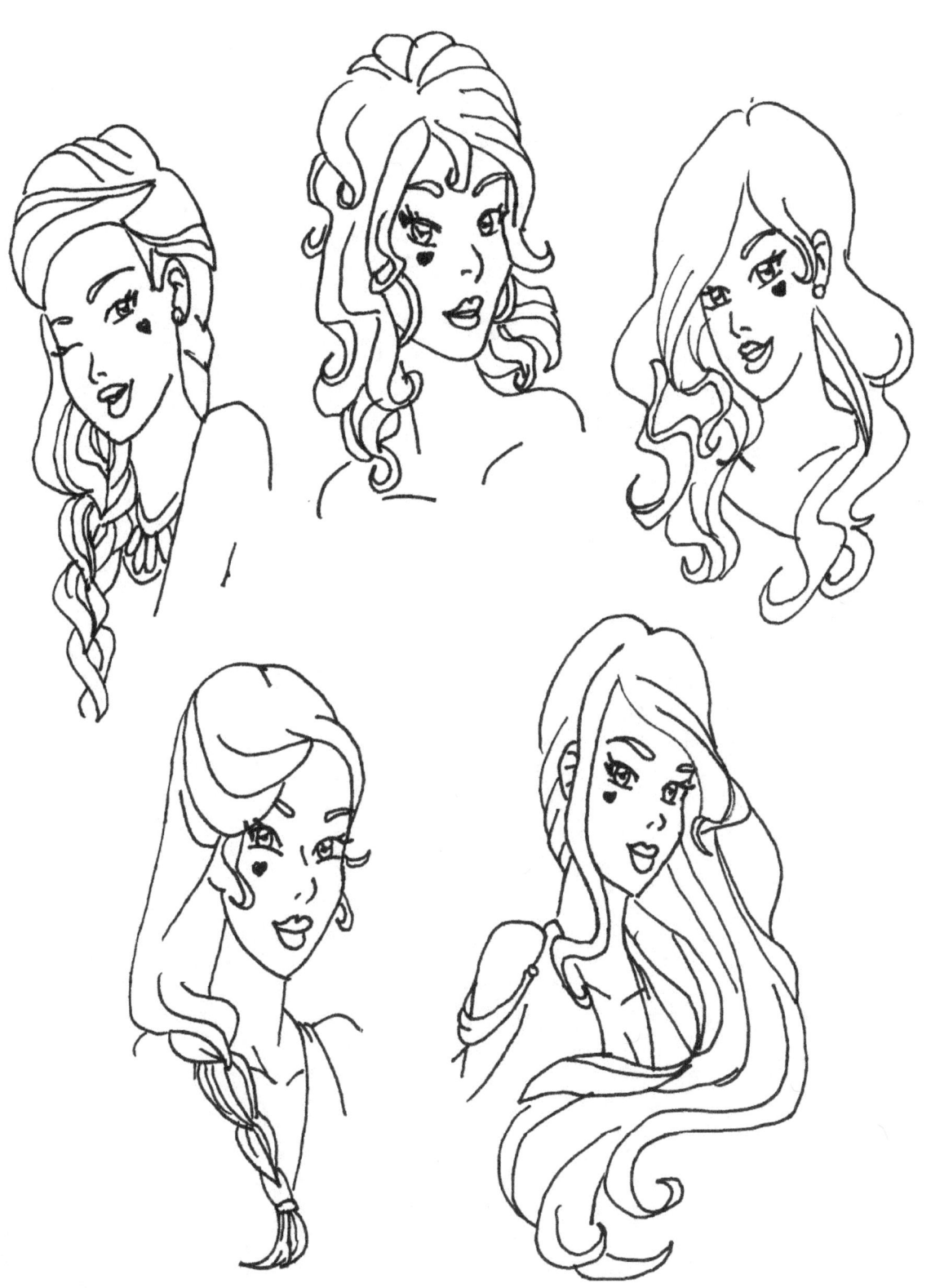

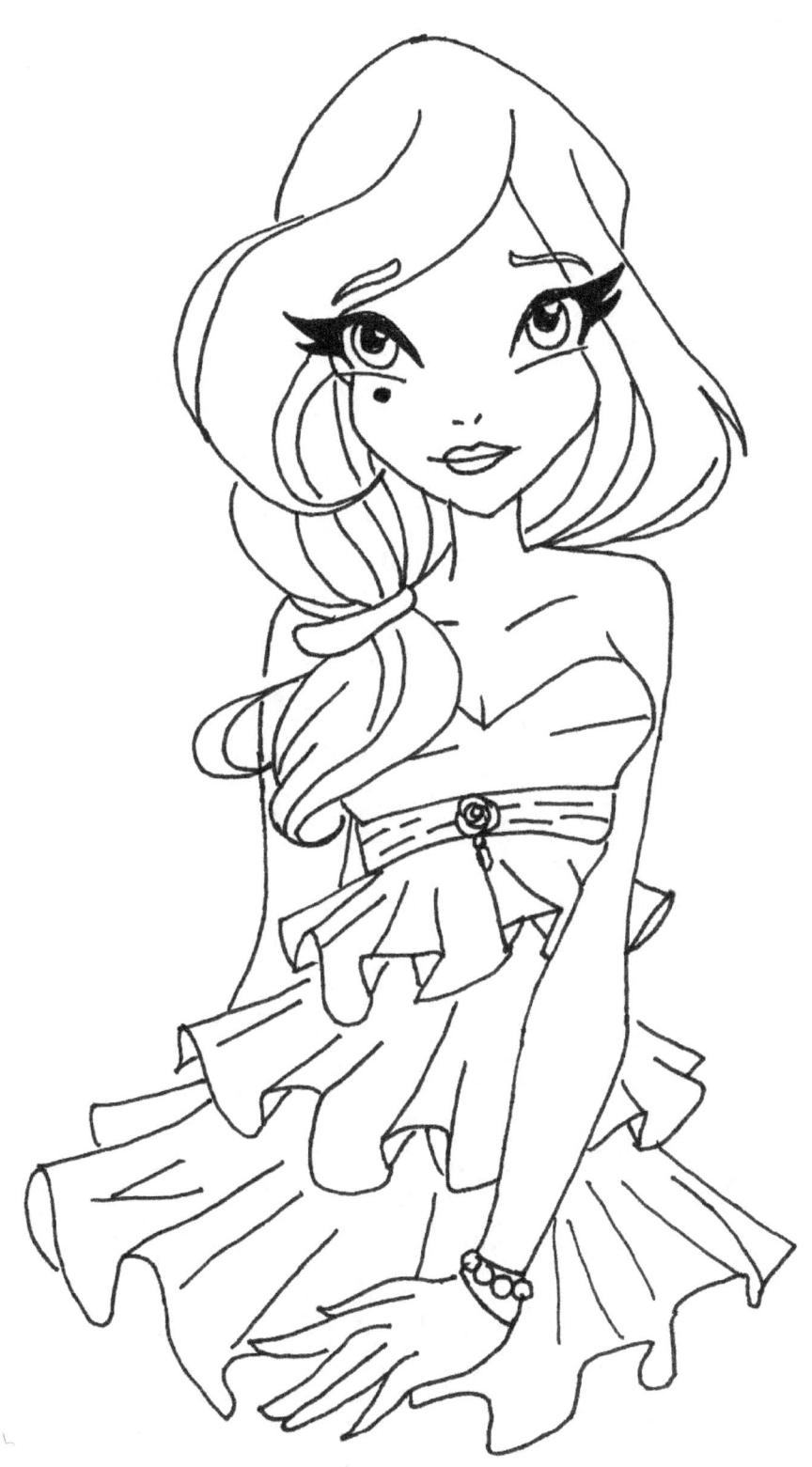

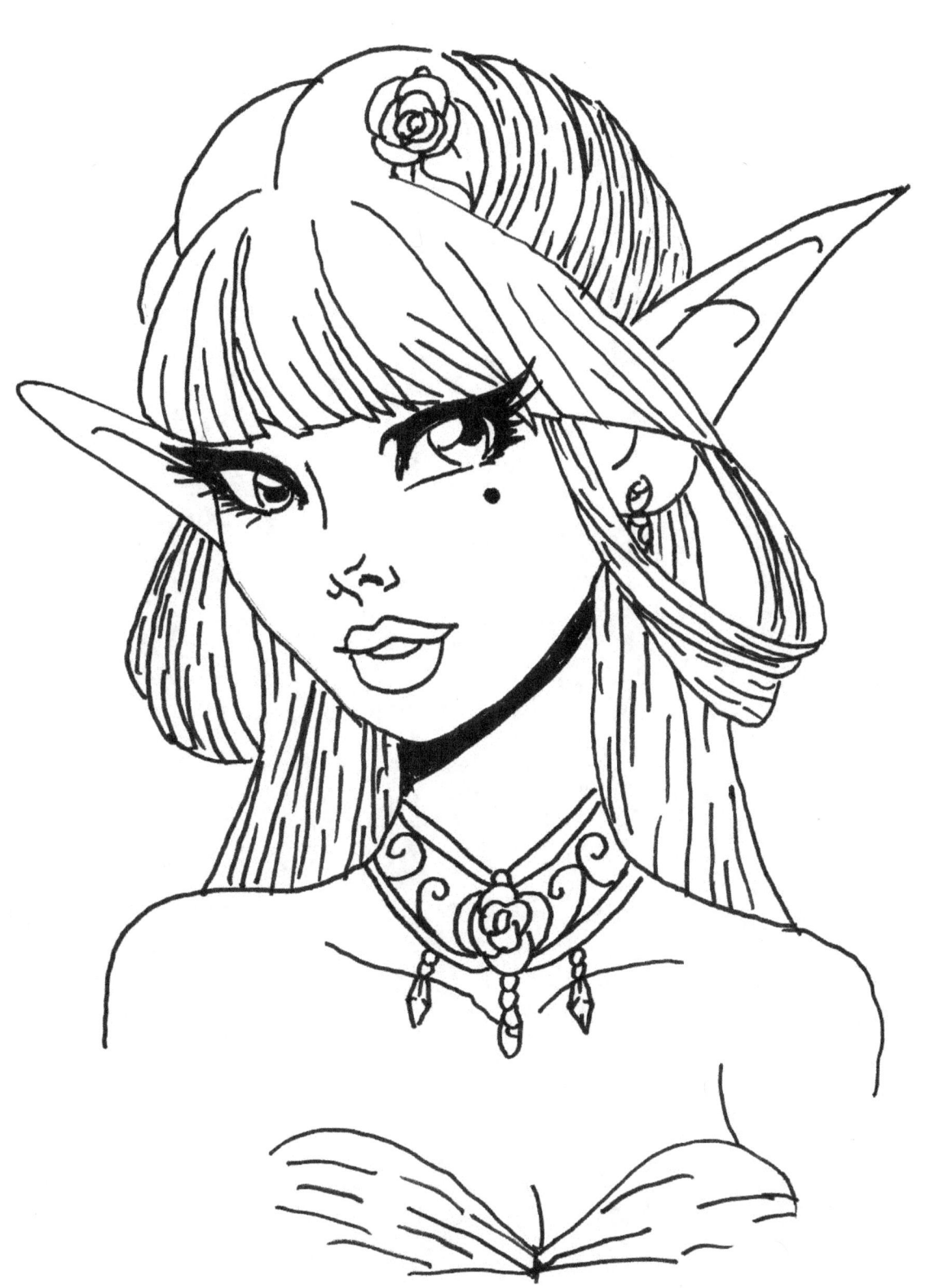

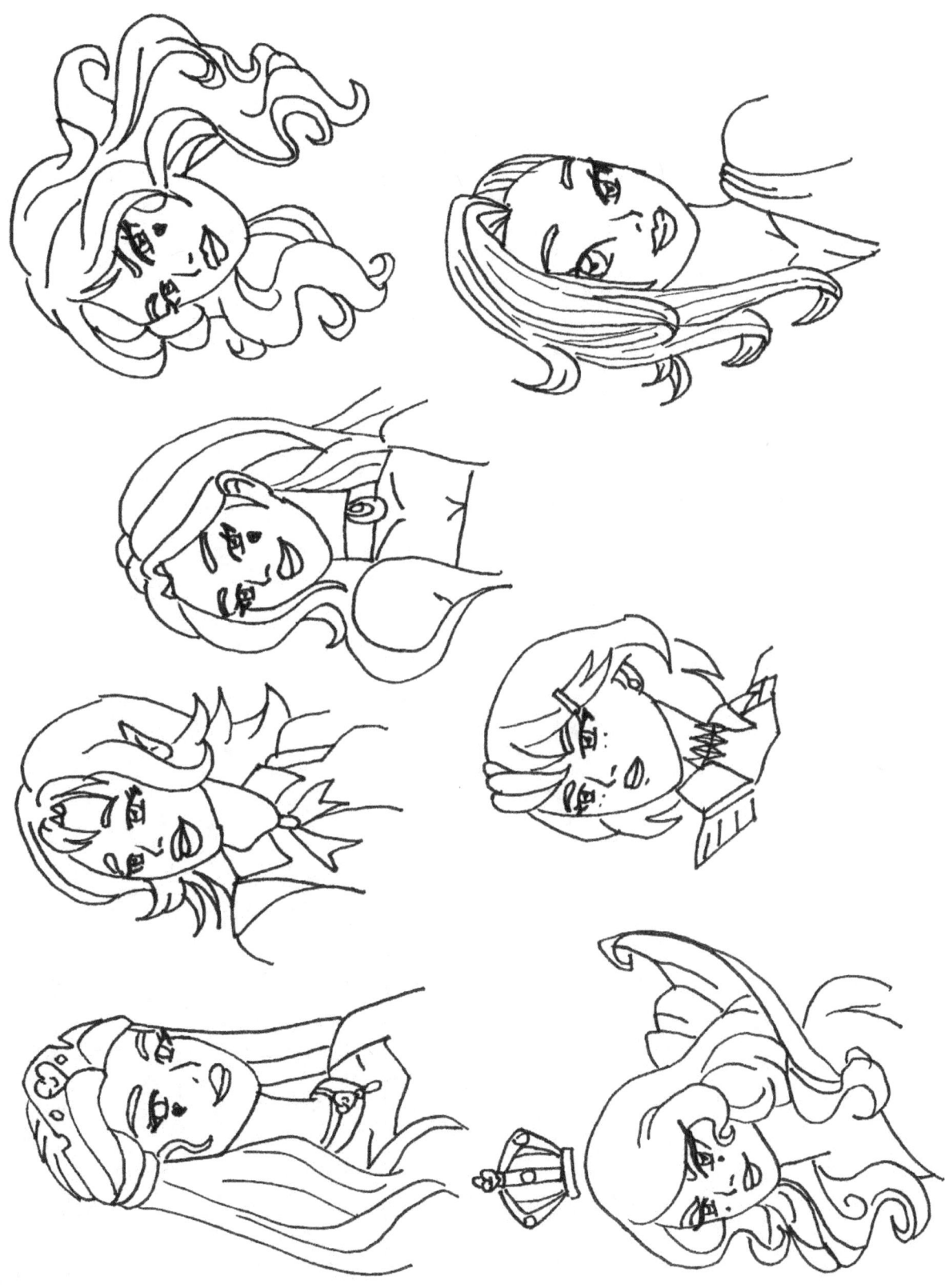

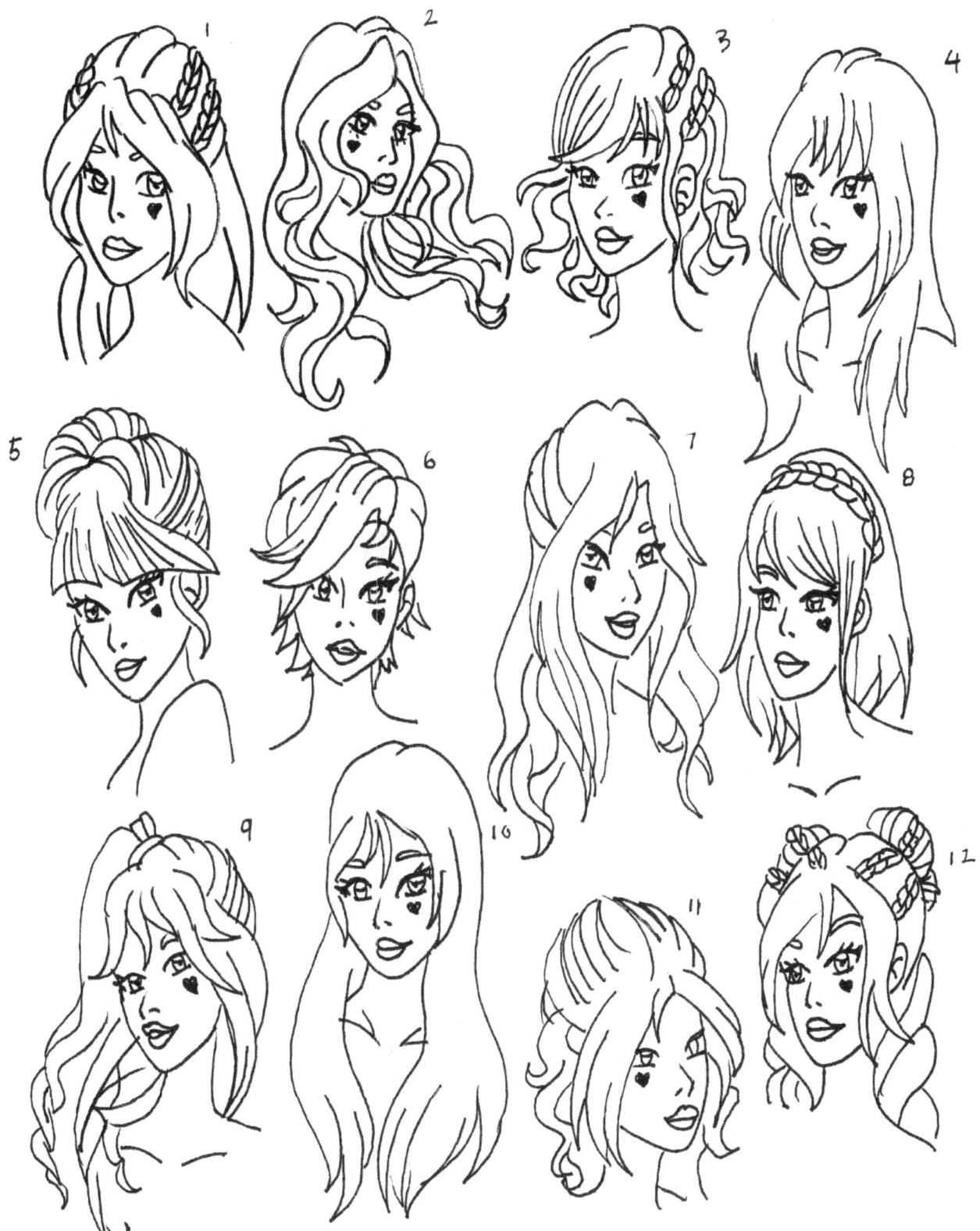

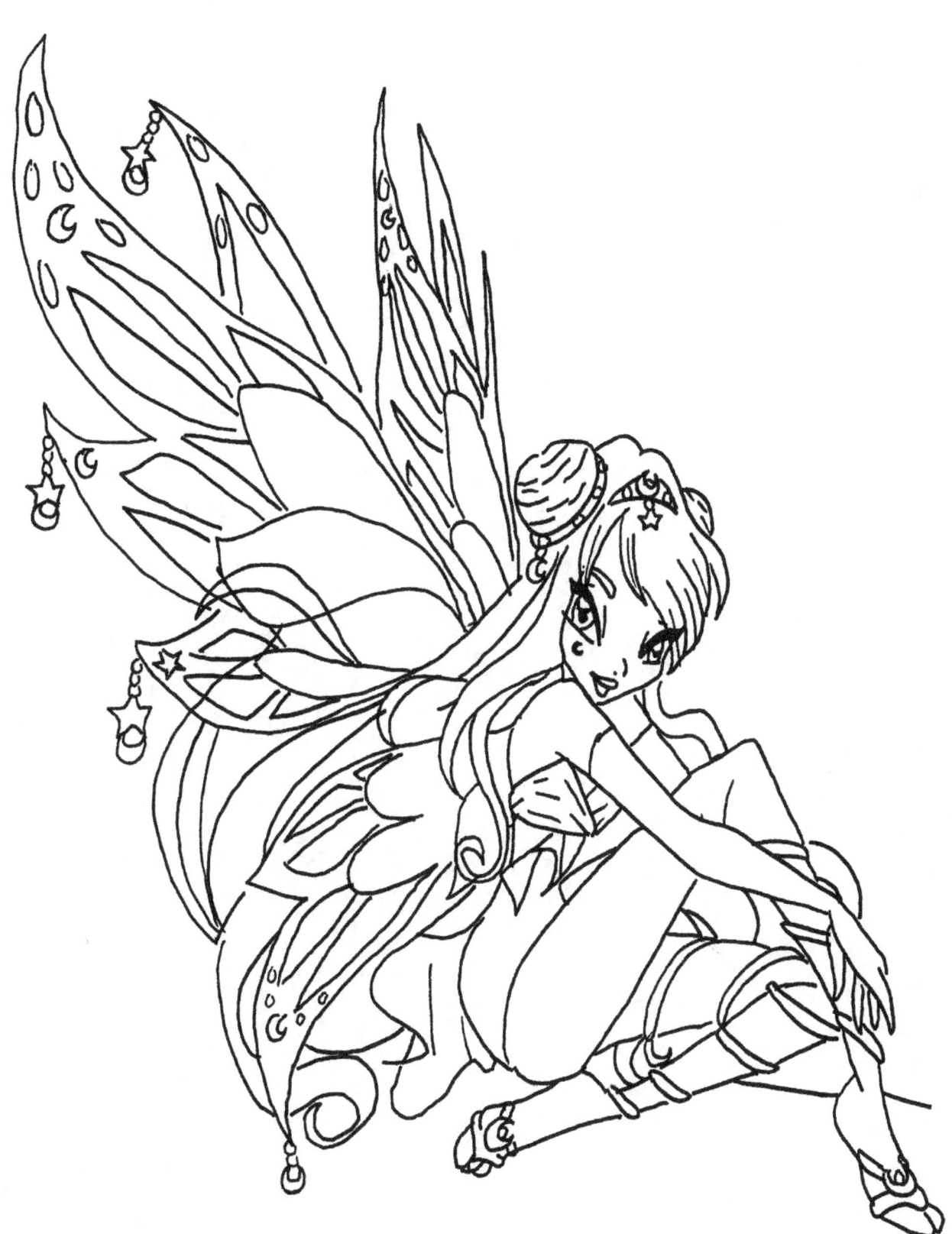

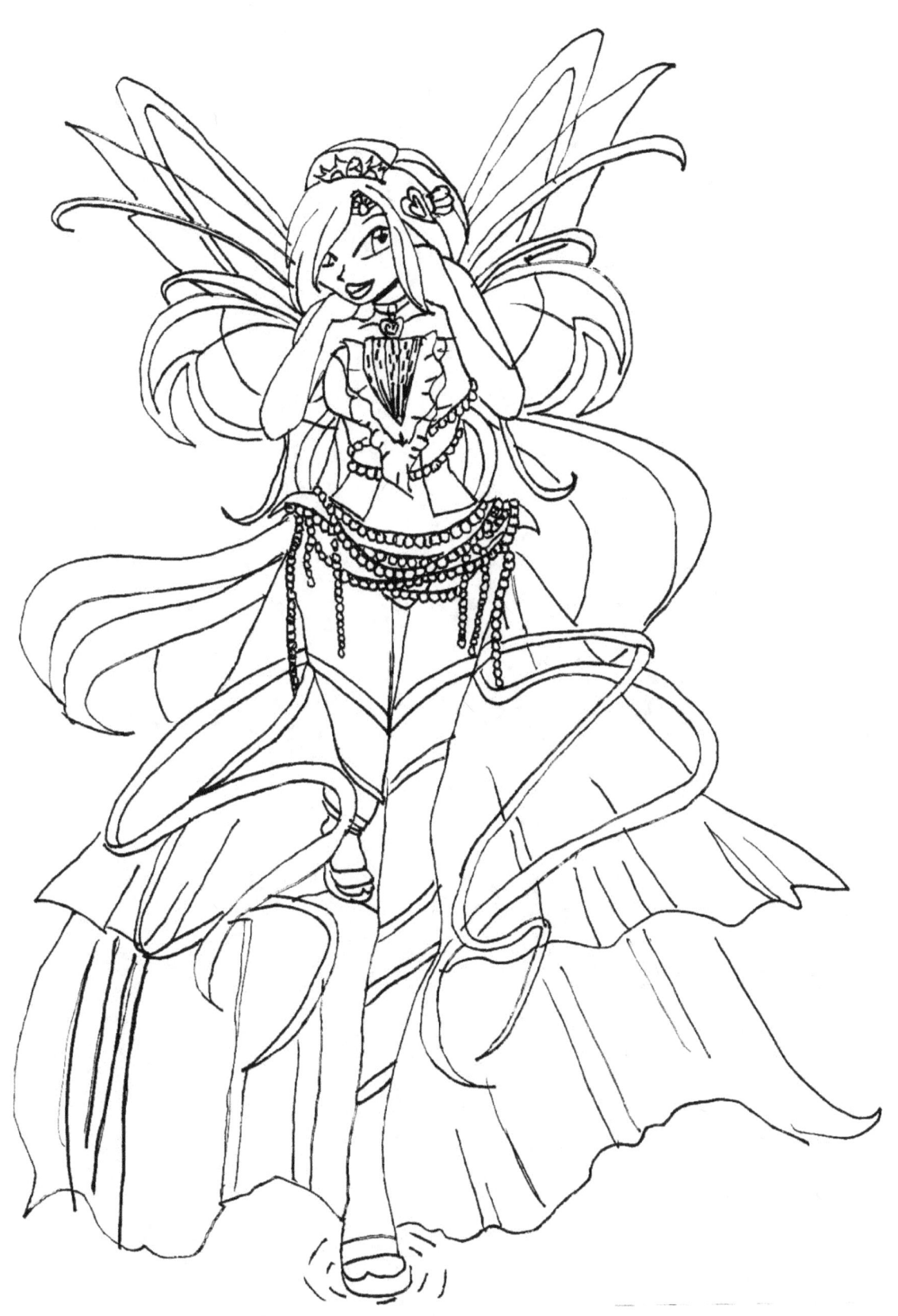

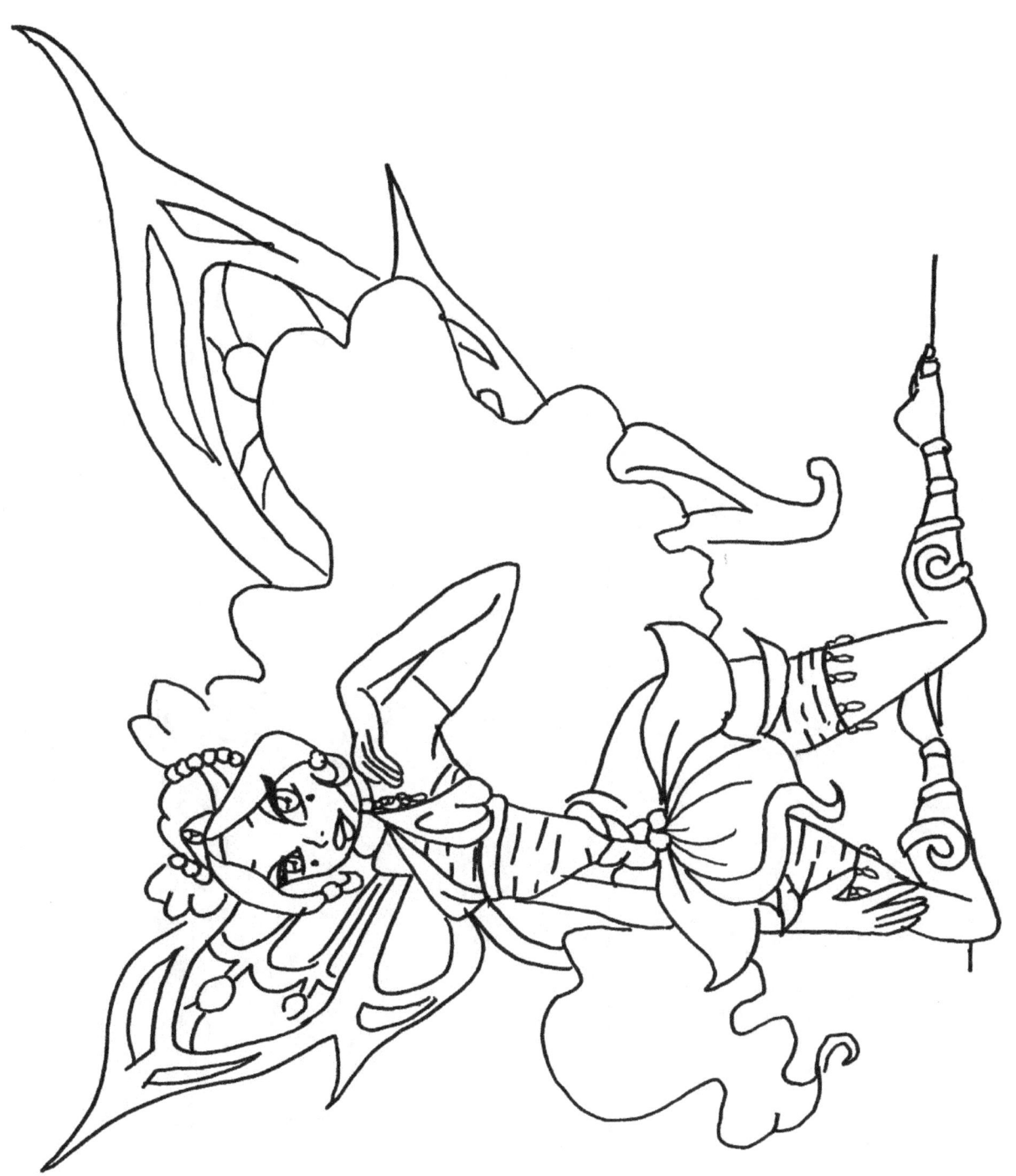

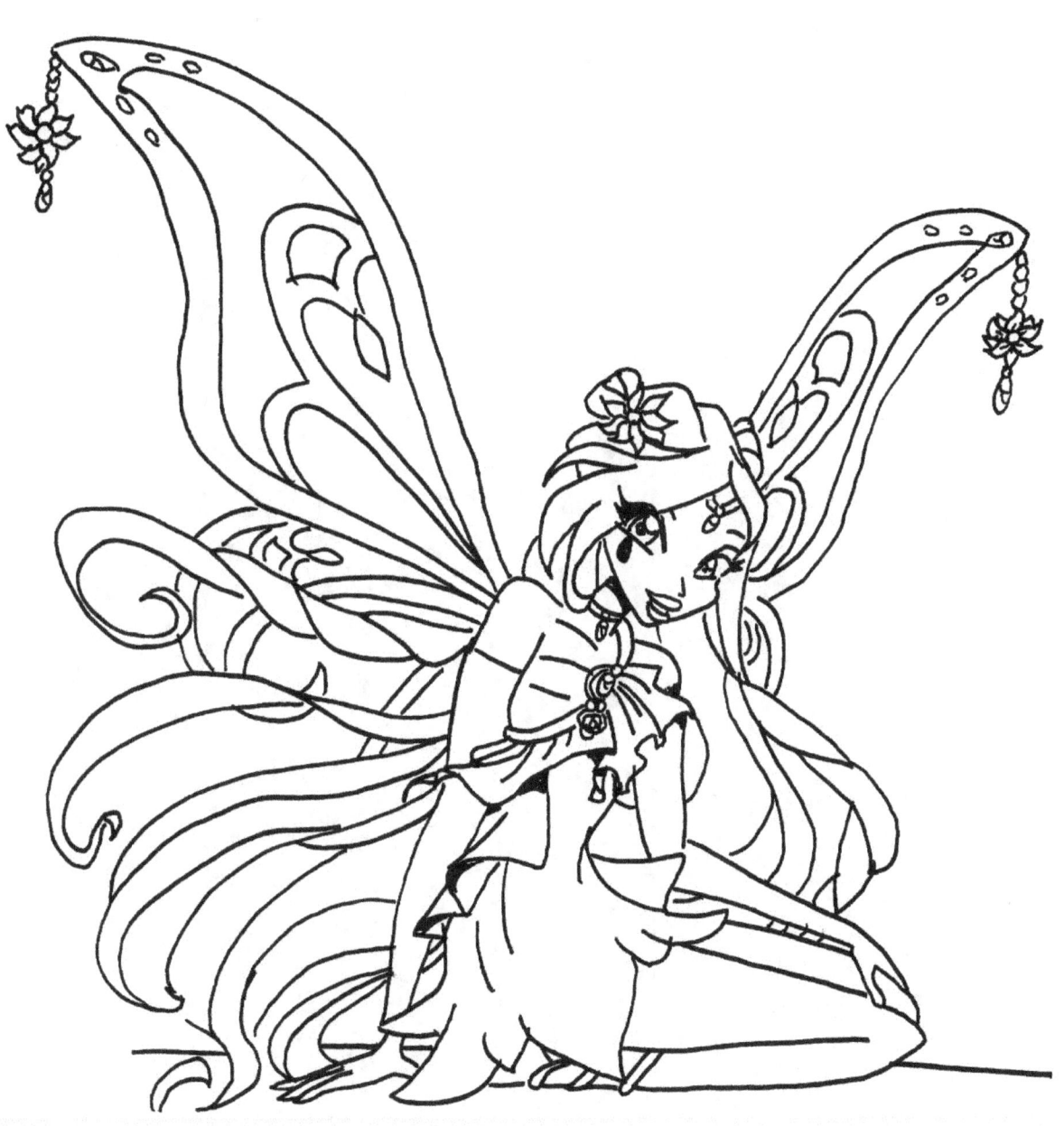

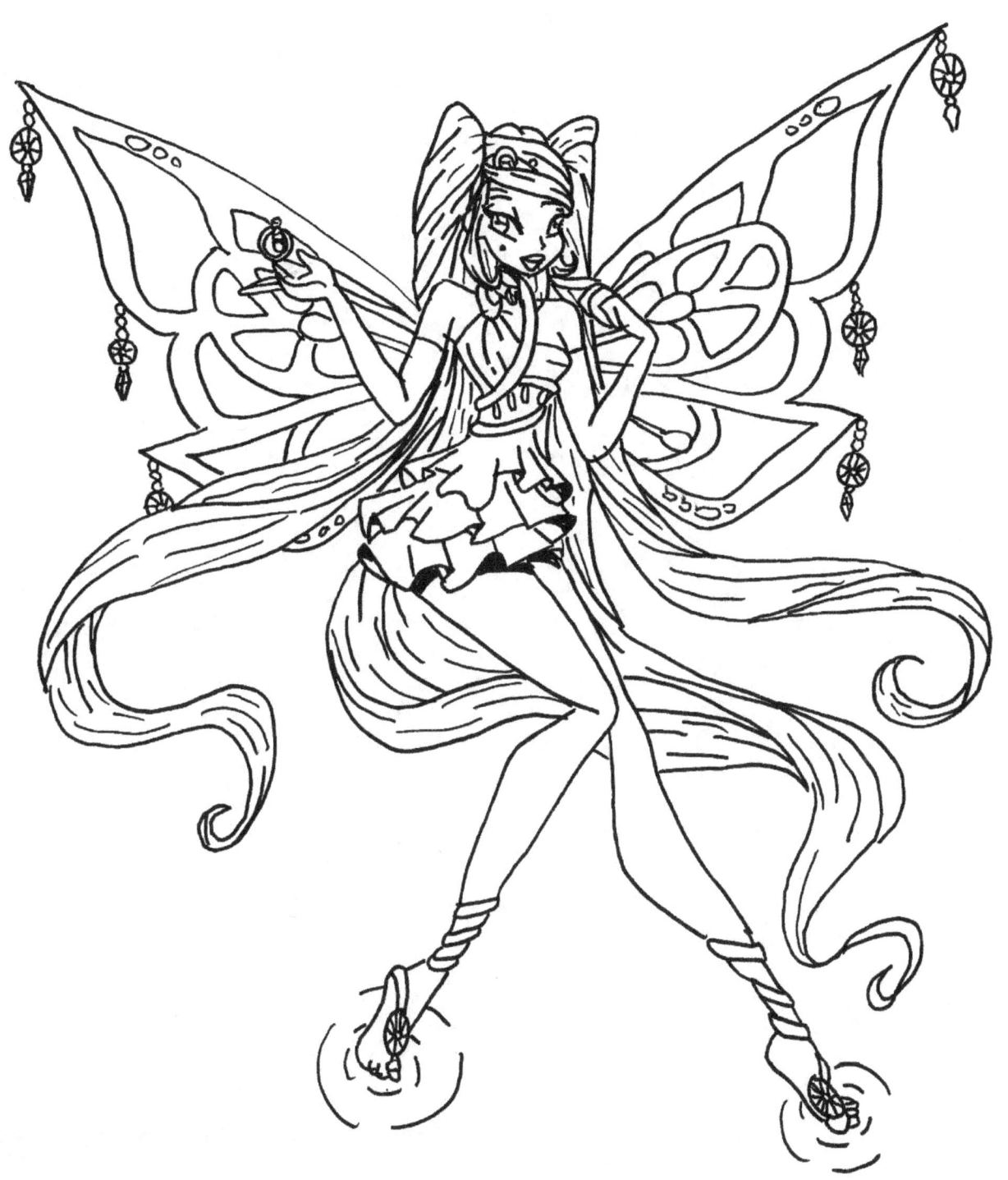

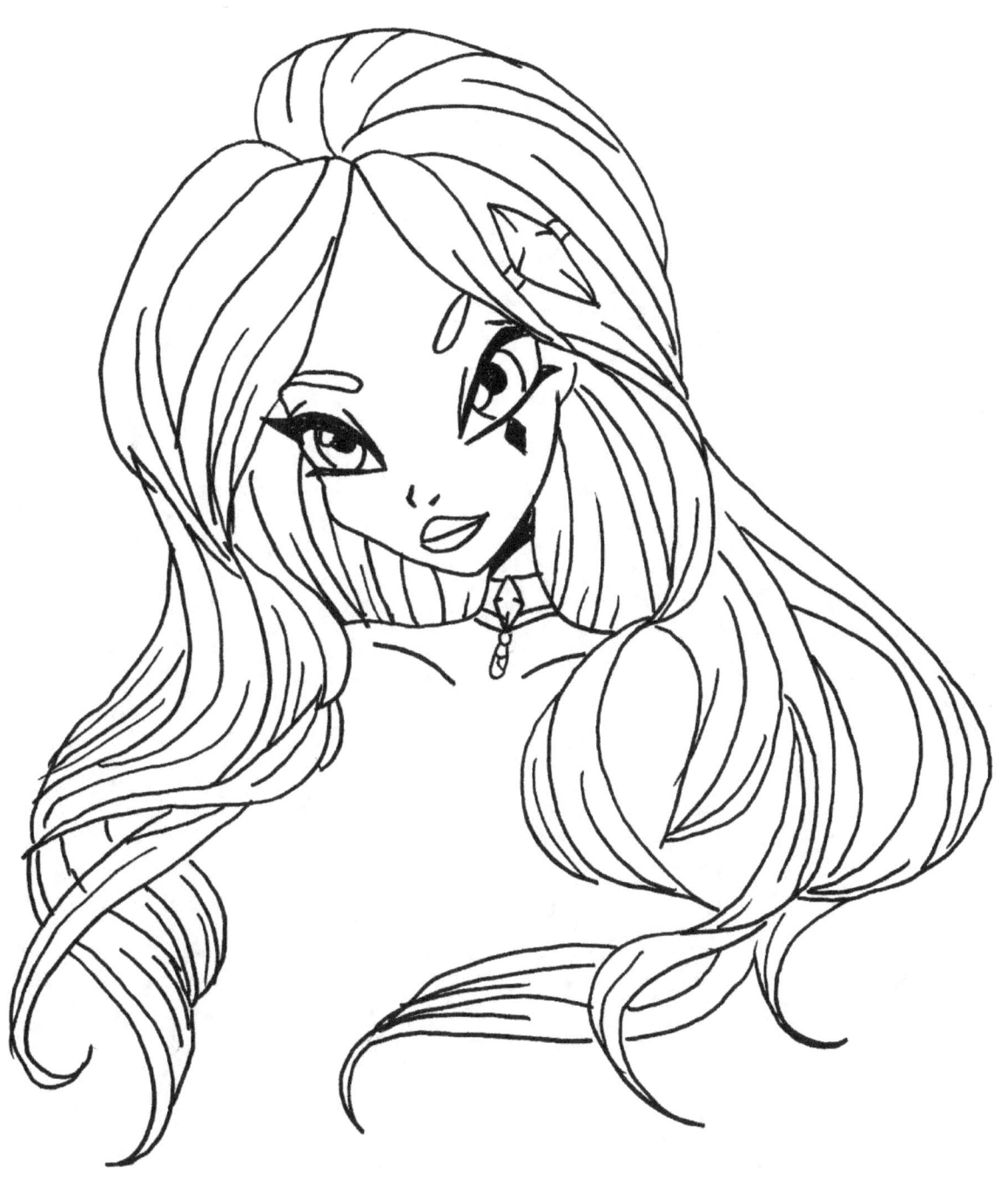

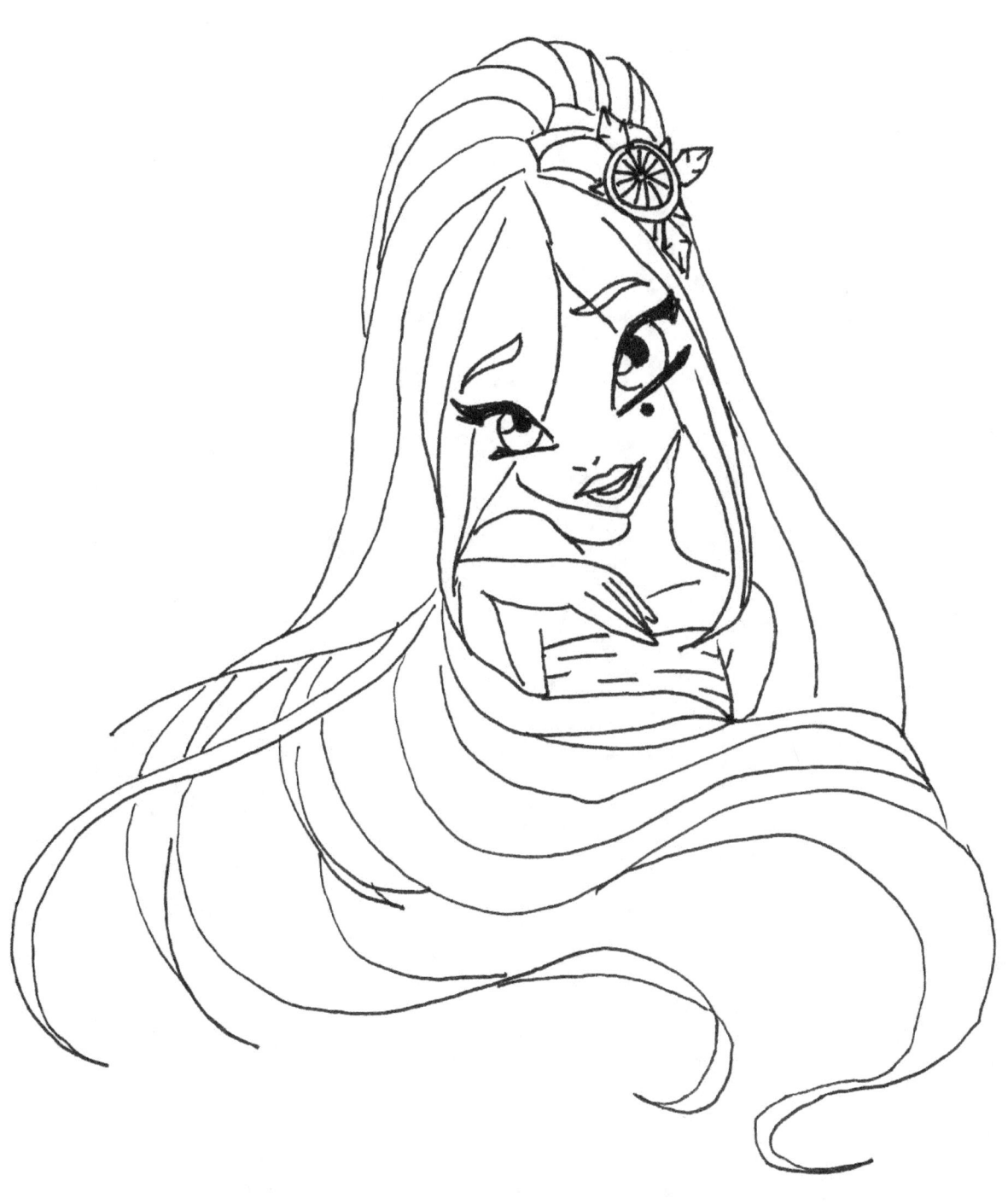

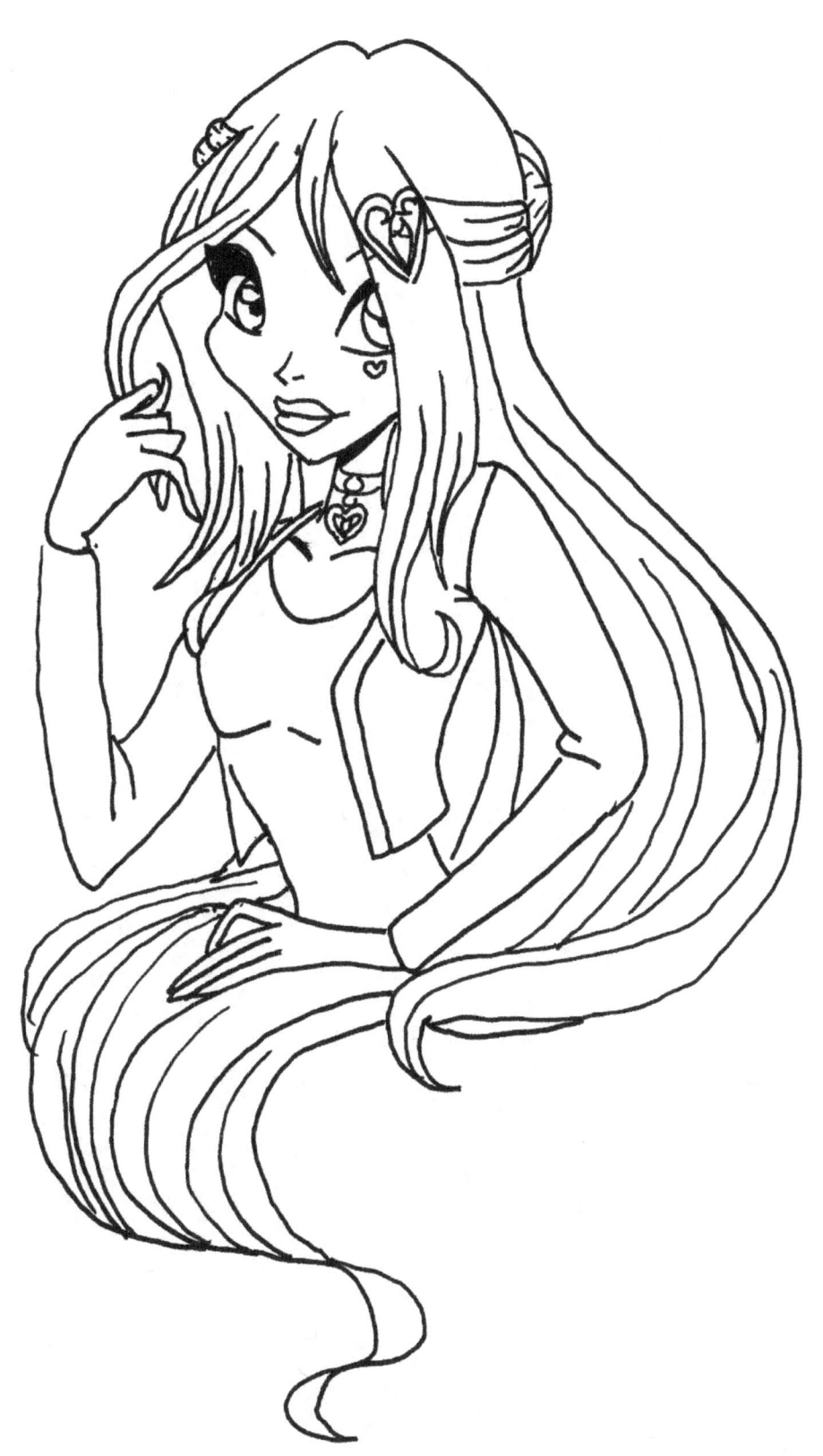

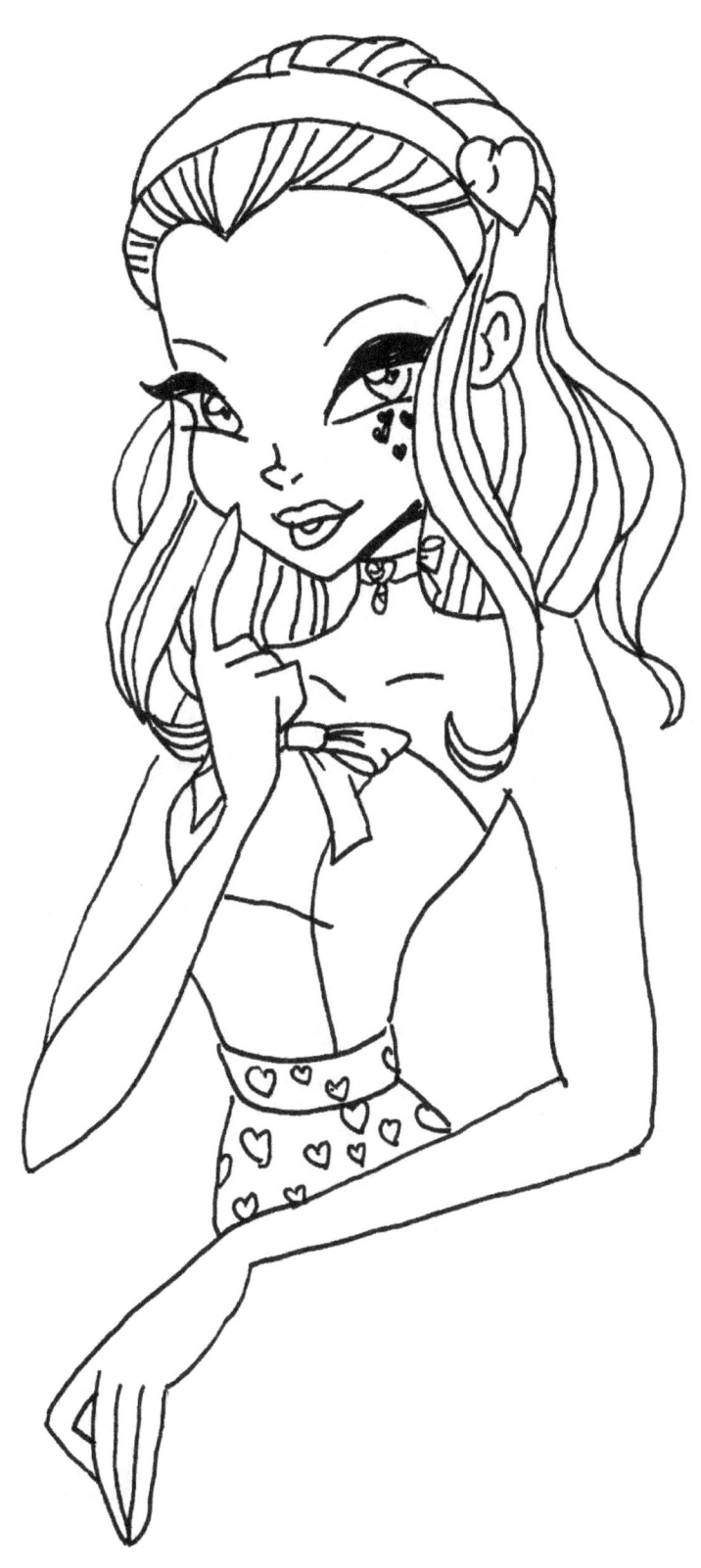

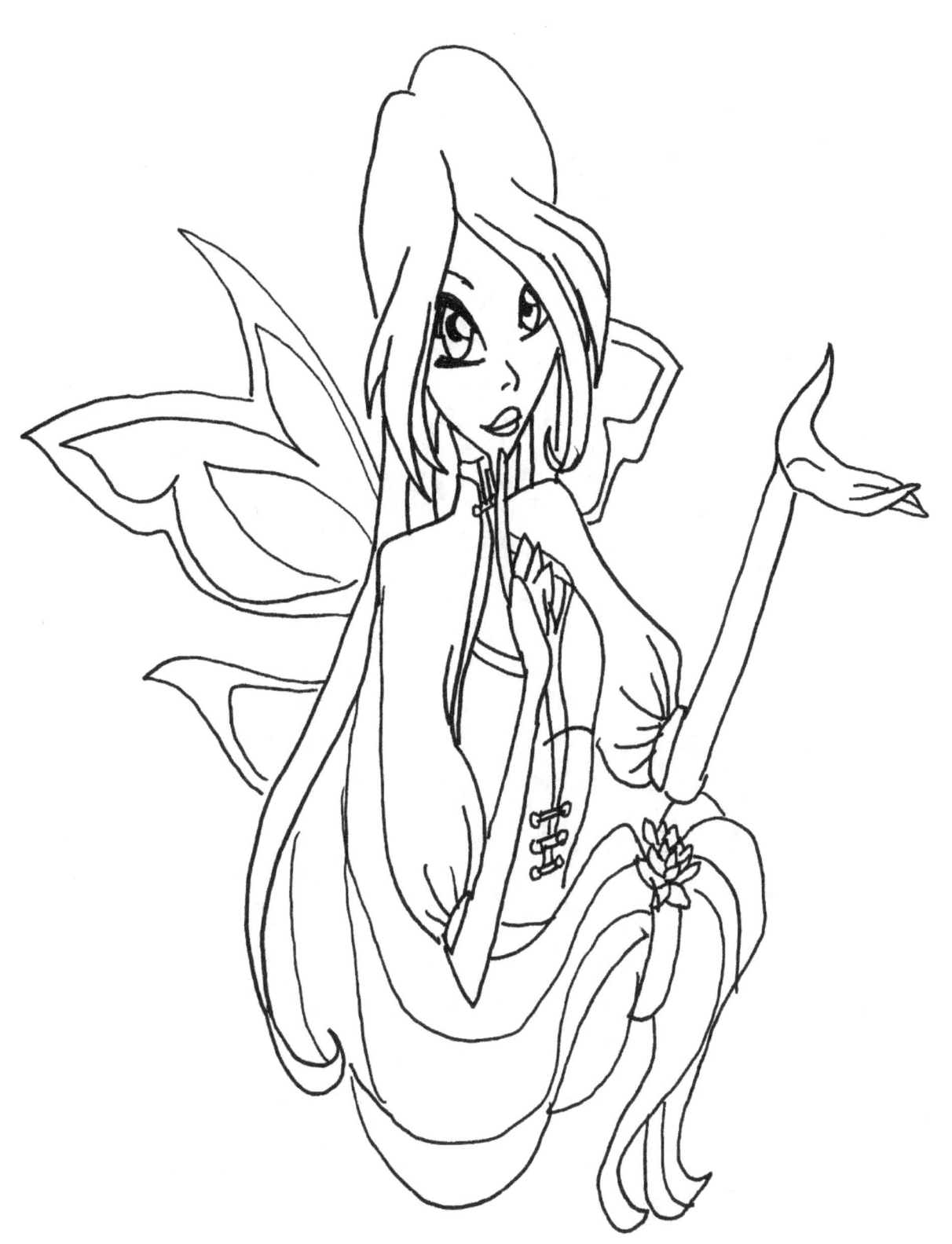

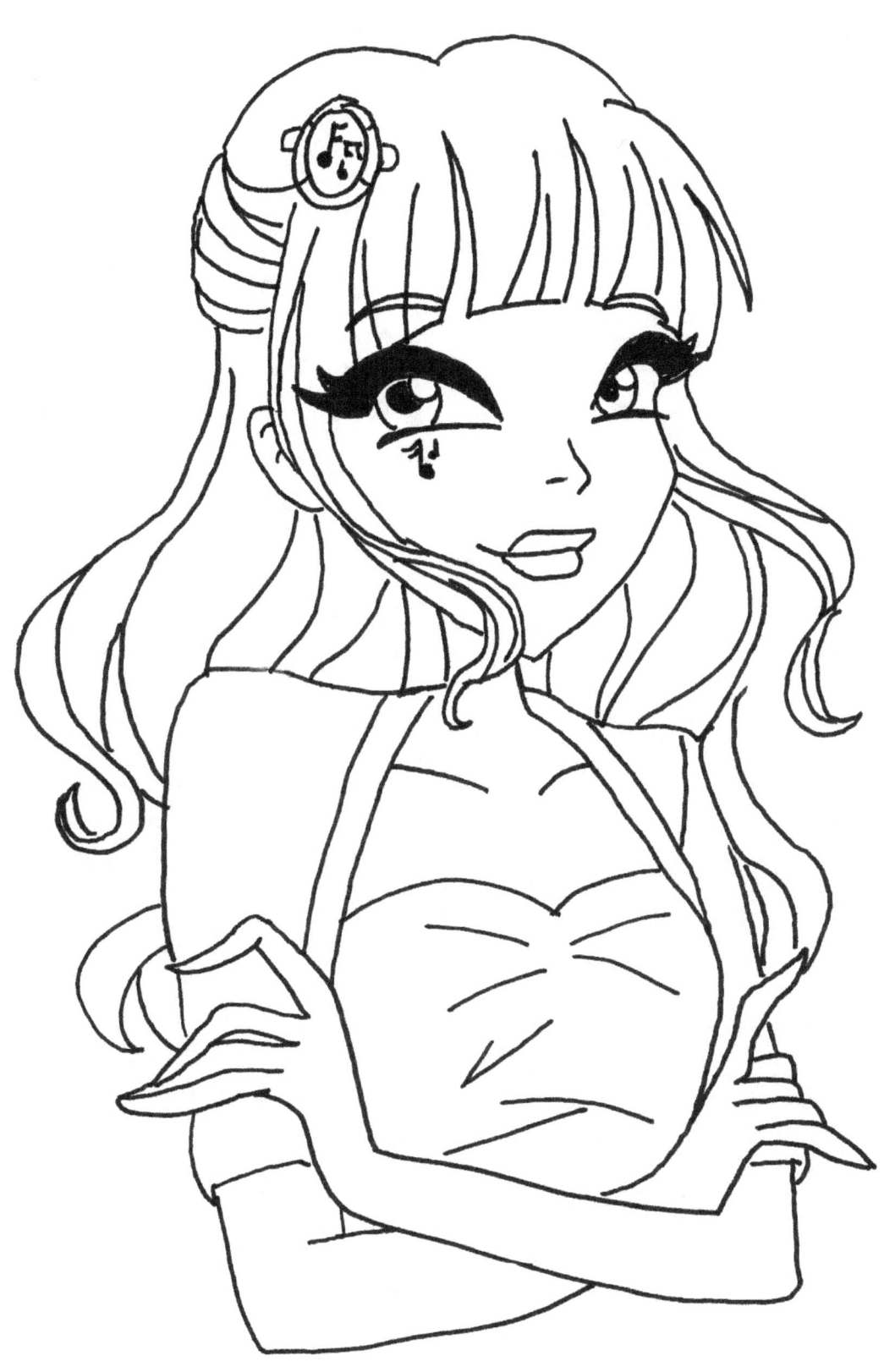

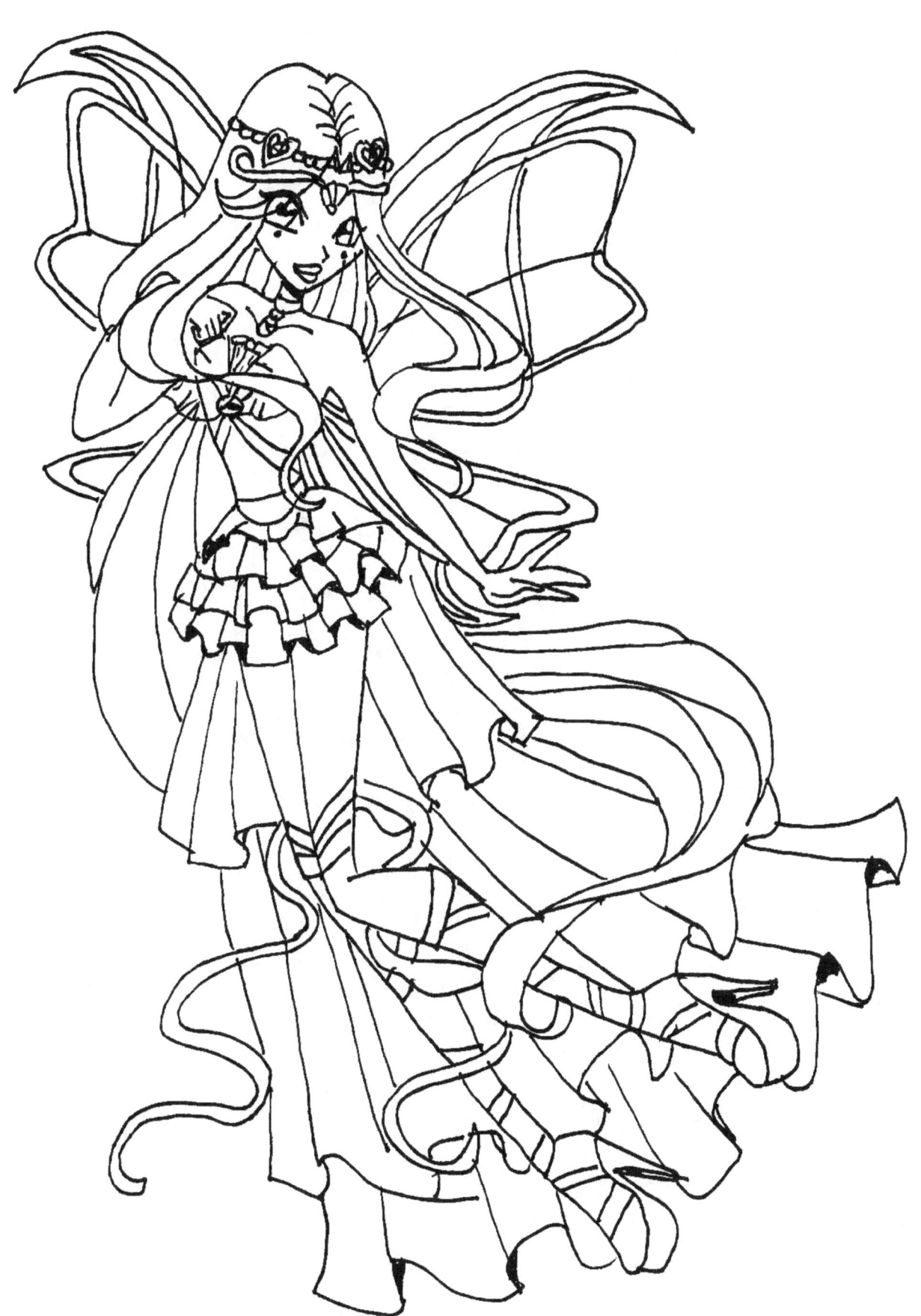

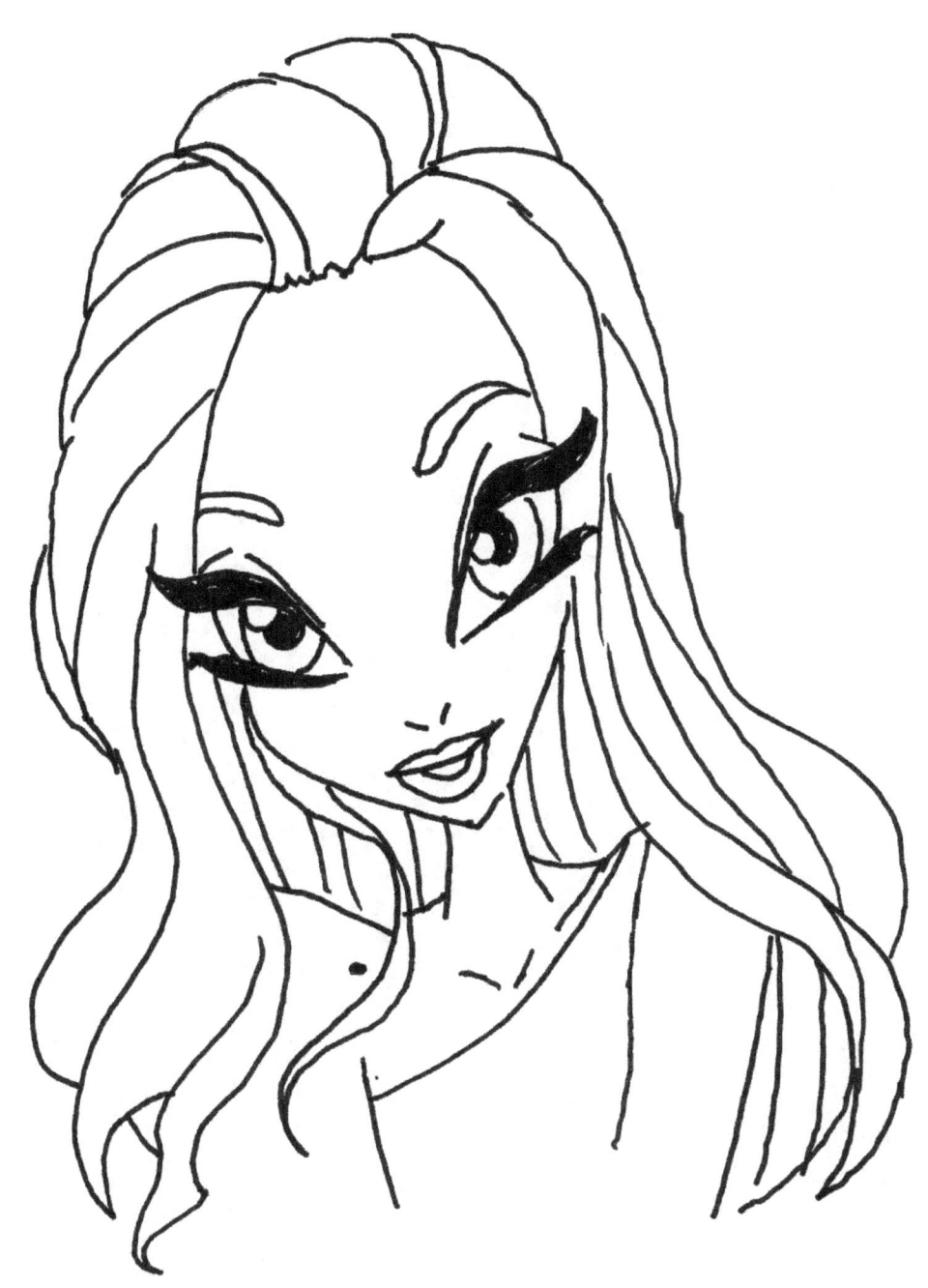

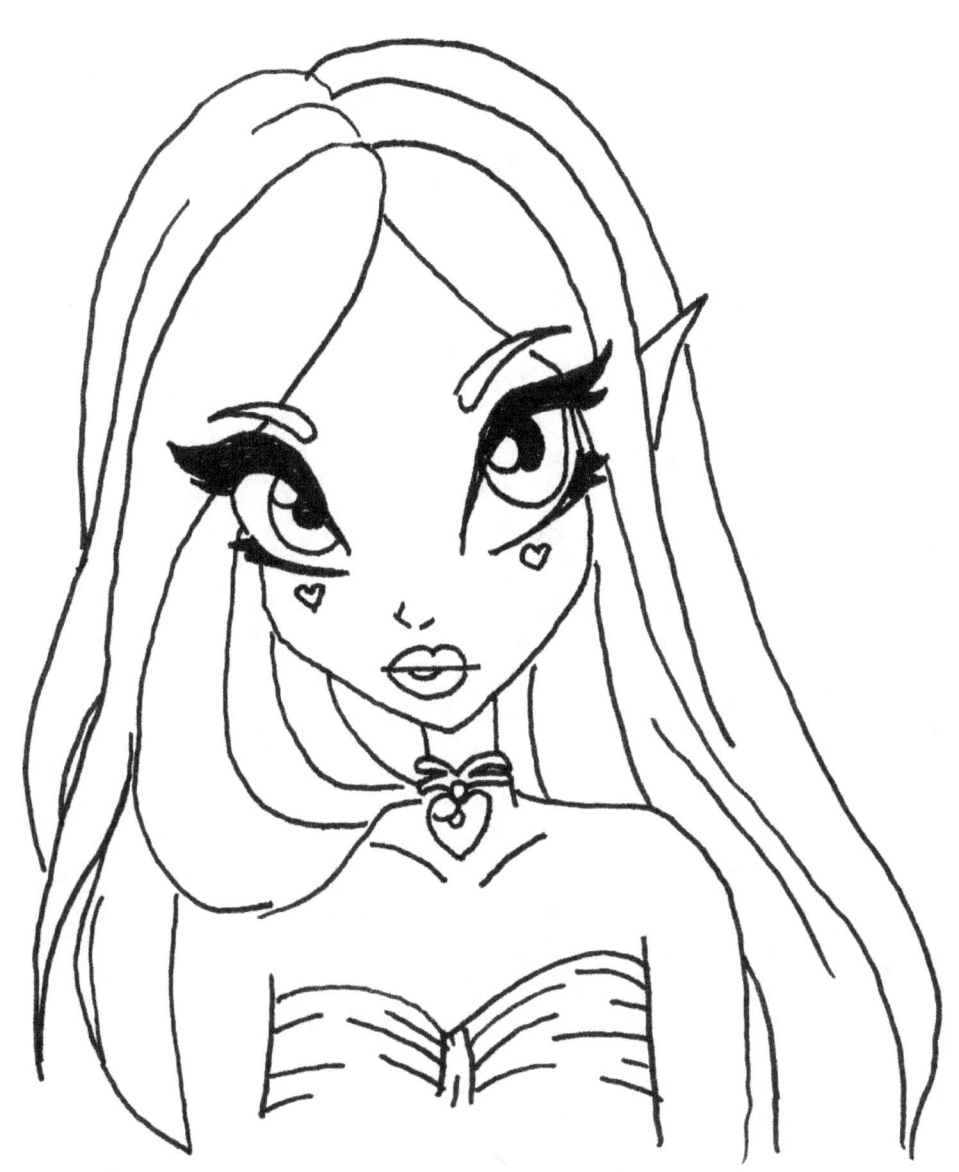

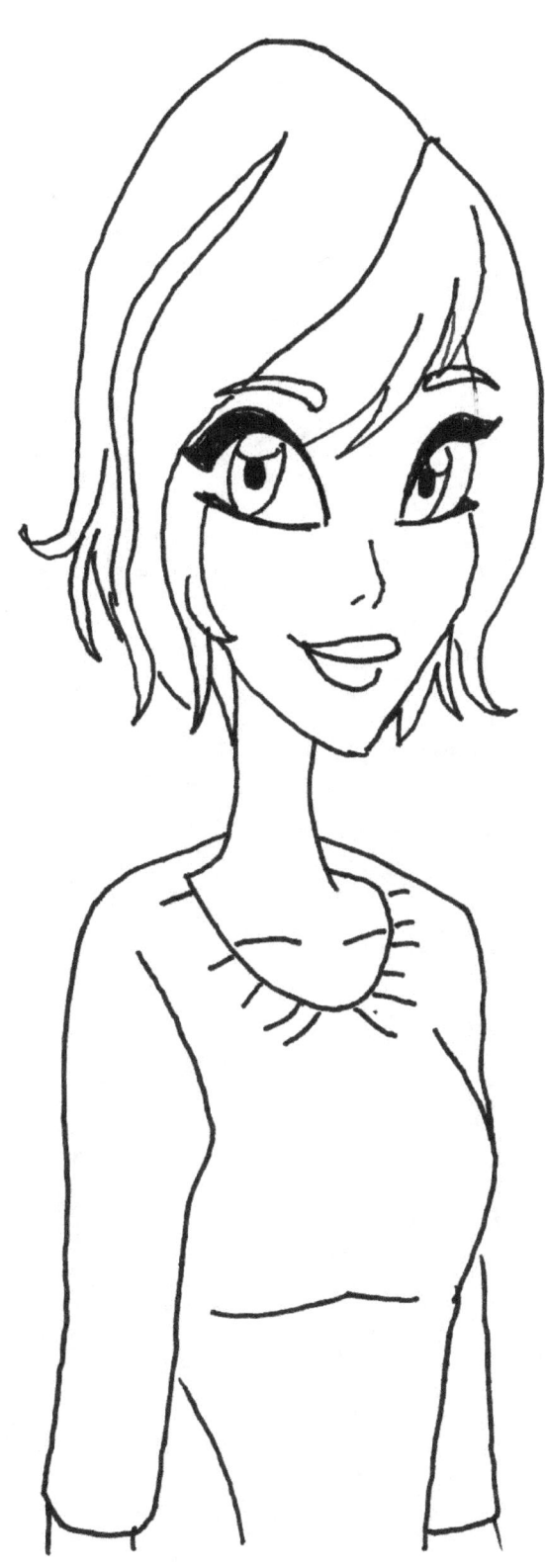